Teaching Your Child HOW TO PRAY

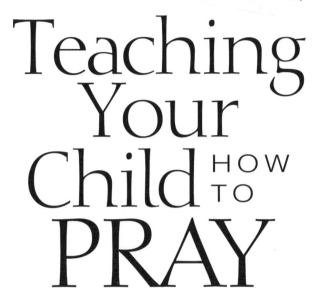

FOCUS ON THE FAMILY®

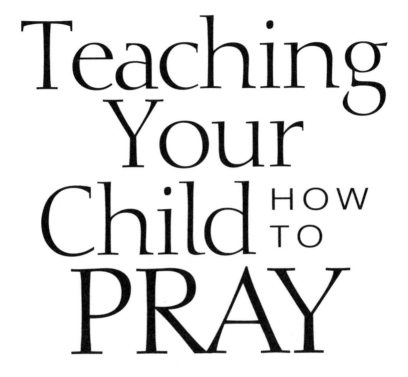

Teaching Your Child How to PRAY

RICK OSBORNE

MOODY PRESS
CHICAGO

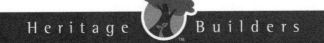

Heritage Builders™

To my three children,
Danica, Sarah, and Joshua,
who make the job of being a parent
a lot of fun, as they add laughter
and wonder to my life every day.

Many thanks to Christie Bowler, my on-staff editor who worked very hard to even out the bumps in my writing. A special thank you to Adeline Griffith, Jim Vincent, Dave DeWit, and Ed van der Maas for their suggestions and help with this book. And also thanks to Terry van Roon for his wonderful page design and to Andrew Jaster for his work in desktop.

ISBN: 0-8024-8493-X

1 3 5 7 9 10 8 6 4 2

Printed in the United States of America

Contents

Foreword

The song is wonderfully true: "Jesus loves the little children, all the children of the world!"

Yes, "They are precious in His sight." And how it must delight His great heart of love when one of these little ones looks to Him in innocent, childlike faith, and prays—or talks with Him. Surely, a little child's prayer of faith will gain God's ear faster than a prayer of lesser faith by a great theologian.

Conversely, how it must grieve God's heart when, because of their upbringing, little children live oblivious to His reality, never knowing of His love and presence, never tapping into the infinite repository of His limitless love and resources.

I know the importance and power of prayer. It has been the foundation of my life and ministry with Bill since before we cofounded Campus Crusade for Christ in 1951, and more recently the Women Today International ministry, which I founded. I have seen the awesome power of prayer when I served for nine years as Chairman of the National Day of Prayer Task Force, which helped marshal prayer throughout America.

By God's grace, Campus Crusade for Christ now has more than 16,000 full-time staff and 200,000 trained volunteers and associates in more than 172 countries. We pray without ceasing, and twice yearly the staff meets all over the world for a full day of prayer together. In addition, we have been extensively involved with the worldwide fasting and prayer movement. Also, in my official National Day of Prayer efforts, we coordinated the prayers of many thousands in cities throughout the nation.

God has allowed me to see answers to big prayers, in big numbers, by big people. Thankfully, He heard and answered them. However, absolutely none of them has been more powerful, or more touching, or more meaningful than those prayers said by our children and grandchildren when they were little, on our knees together, or on my lap.

As children, they didn't know anything about the great theological questions and debates of the day, and could not have cared less. They were not interested in the theoretical, or the abstract. Their world demanded the concrete. They only knew that God was real, that Jesus loved them and died for them, and that He carefully listened to what they had to say.

Simplicity. Reality. Faith. Results. Oh, how we sophisticated adults could learn from the children, "for of such is the kingdom of God."

Training up children in the way they should go, to know and follow God, is the most responsible job in the universe. Teaching them to pray is one of the most important parts of that training process. The faithful prayers of these little ones can actually change the universe—and their world.

Rick Osborne has done a masterful job of bringing together important principles and outstanding guidelines in *Teaching Your Child How to Pray*.

Combined with the reader's prayers, I believe the Lord will greatly use this book to revolutionize and strengthen the spiritual lives of their children, providing them a solid foundation, from which, the Lord promises in His Word, they "will not depart" (Proverbs 22:6, NKJV).

God's ear is waiting.

VONETTE BRIGHT
Founder of
National Day of Prayer Task Force

PART 1

"Get Ready"

We tend to look at prayer as an aid to our lives, but God intended it to be the foundation.

We learn to pray as adults, with the goal being to change things. But God intended us to learn to pray as children and get it right from the start.

A small boy, almost six years old, lay wide awake in his bed dreaming of owning his own pocketknife. He wanted to whittle. He imagined that he could carve out a pair of crutches for a crippled boy he knew so that the boy could play with the other children.

It was hard times in the deep South. Lying in that small bed in a one-room cabin tucked away in the woods, the boy knew it was an impossible wish. But as he thought, he remembered the Father who could give him the knife he needed. He simply prayed and asked his Father for what he wanted. That night he dreamed of a broken and partially eaten watermelon that lay at the foot of some cornstalks. Sticking into the watermelon was the object of his prayer: a black-handled knife.

First light found the boy racing over fences and through fields to reach the spot he had seen in his dream. When he arrived at his destination, there were the cornstalks, the watermelon, and the black-handled knife! The boy didn't consider what had happened unusual or extraordinary; his Father had simply answered his prayer. All his life, it seemed to this boy that to talk to God and ask for wisdom, help, and guidance was the natural thing to do.

The boy, George Washington Carver, grew up to become a distinguished agricultural chemist whose accomplishments changed the world. (His story is detailed at the end of this section.) But George would view his notable accomplishments as he viewed the black-handled knife: with humble gratitude toward God. For with the pocketknife the young boy had seen a prayer answered and much more: He had begun to walk and talk with God.

Just as George did, our children can learn about a faithful, caring God when they learn how to pray. In part 1 we will see how we can "get ready" to help our children to pray, primarily through understanding the foundational reasons for teaching them to pray and through seeing the benefits prayer will bring to them.

To make this book as practical as possible, in each chapter we have provided questions for reflection and discussion, along with some suggested activities you can do with your children. At the end of each chapter we have also suggested some things you might want to pray about and have given a sample prayer your children can use as a starting point.

Giving Our Children the Best

GOD, COULD YOU PLEASE GET MY DAD TO TAKE ME TO
MOVIES AND GAMES EVERY WEEK, TO PLAY CATCH AND
HIDE-AND-GO-SEEK MORE OFTEN, TO NEVER GET MAD
AT ME, BUY ME MORE CANDY...

Giving Our Children the Best

Half an hour of prayer, morning or evening, every day, may be a greater element in shaping our course than all our conduct and all our thought.
P. T. Forsyth

Today, sending our children to school to learn the basics is just a beginning. We want the best for our children, so we make sure we do all we can for them.

We teach our children to ride bikes, skate, swim, and ski. We sign them up early for baseball, soccer, football, hockey, and/or basketball, and we send them to sports camps in the summer. You may offer your children the musical arts: piano, violin, voice lessons, guitar, and, if they must, drums. Also, if you or your children are so inclined, there is dance, ballet, gymnastics, tumbling, and/or trampoline. You can enroll your children in acting, stage, performance classes, and even modeling. And afterward you can find them an agent.

Some parents hire tutors for extra help, take their children to second-language schools after their regular schooling, enroll them in night school or weekend community courses, and/or take them to summer school. They don't do this because their children are behind; they want to help them get ahead.

It may seem funny to see it all listed like this, yet the time spent driving, enrolling children in lessons, attending concerts, practices, games, recitals, and auditions is serious, valuable time. We want our children to develop fully their talents, abilities, and character. We can buy books that will help us teach our children manners, values, virtues, and assertiveness. There are books to teach them how to handle finances, get better grades, discover their personality types, learn business basics, conquer public speaking, and be politicians. (Well, I haven't seen that one yet, but I'm sure it won't be long.)

So, why do we do it? Because we love our children and want the best for them. This is as it should be.

Giving the Very Best: Prayer

As important as all these skills and experiences are, there is something far more important—something that is foundational for all of life, something that will truly equip our children for whatever their futures hold. This something is prayer.

Teaching our children to pray will truly prepare them for life and equip them to face everything life has to offer.

Jesus once scolded the religious leaders because even though they were careful to give exactly 10 percent of their spices to the temple, they were not treating people very well. He wasn't saying they shouldn't give a portion of their spices to God; He was drawing a contrast that highlighted their lack of proper focus. In a similar way, all these things we teach our children are important, and the activities and tasks can better prepare them for life, but, in comparison to the importance and benefit of teaching our children to pray, they are like giving 10 percent of our spices.

Teaching our children to pray will truly prepare them for life and equip them to face everything life has to offer. By teaching them to pray, we will be teaching our children to communicate with the One who is their Creator, Father, Teacher, and Guide—

the One who loves them more than we can imagine.

Teaching our children to pray will put them in touch with the Father who not only wants the best for them but who knows what that best is and has the power and resources to deliver. Jesus compared our ability to give to our children to God's ability when He said, "If you then, though you are evil, know how to give good gifts to your children, how much more will your Father in heaven give good gifts to those who ask him!" (Matthew 7:11).

A recent Gallup survey published in *Parenting* magazine revealed that about 65 percent of parents pray with their children before bed and at mealtimes.[1] This suggests that as parents we have a heart for prayer and acknowledge prayer's importance. But, although bedtime and mealtime are great places to start, teaching a child to pray must go beyond those times.

Reflections

1. What role does prayer play in your family's life? In your relationships with your children?

    _____

    _____

    _____

2. What are some things you want for your children? How can teaching them about prayer help them get those things?

    _____

    _____

    _____

The Benefits of Prayer Lessons

When my wife, Elaine, and I enrolled our daughters in violin, we considered the benefits first: (1) learning music basics while young seemed easier for them, and the learning would become natural; (2) the classes would be fun and rewarding and would give our daughters an appreciation for music; (3) the lessons would help them to learn the discipline that regular practice brings.

Every parent wants to see the success and promotion of their children. As an audience, we constantly rejoice over Cinderella stories. The low, humble but beautiful, and often sweet-spirited child is whisked away from trouble in Plainsville and given a place among royalty. Childhood stories from *Rumpelstiltskin* to *The Prince and the Pauper* to Disney's recent adaptations of *Beauty and the Beast*, *The Little Mermaid*, and *Aladdin* all carry this familiar theme.

This is closer to reality than you might think for we have an invitation from the King of all kings for our children to go to heaven—the ultimate palace. Here all can receive status as part of the royal family of God. But this invitation to heaven is not simply to attend. It's an invitation to sit, talk with, and get to know the One who is all-powerful and in charge of everything. It's an invitation for our children to become permanent members of that family and enjoy its benefits. And membership with its benefits begins before their arrival in heaven; it begins right here on earth.

Jesus said, "Let the little children come to me, and do not hinder them, for the kingdom of God belongs to such as these" (Mark 10:14).

God's offer to all—children and adults—to enter His kingdom includes knowing and experiencing God's presence. Consider these verses:

> "Then you will call upon me and come and pray to me, and I will listen to you. You will seek me and find me when you seek me with all your heart. I will be found by you," declares the LORD. (Jeremiah 29:12–14)

> Jesus replied, "If anyone loves me, he will obey my teaching. My Father will love him, and we will come to him and make our home with him." (John 14:23; see also Jeremiah 24:7 and James 4:8)

When we teach our children not only to pray but to have prayer as part of the *foundation* of their lives and who they are, we give them the ultimate gifts, benefits, and blessings that life has to offer: an audience with and the friendship of God.

Let's consider prayer in a way similar to how we consider music lessons. What advantages does a regular and healthy prayer life bring to our children? Many! The advantages flow out of that relationship with God. The Bible, God's Word, clearly describes several of these benefits, ranging from a better inner life to promotion and honor.

1. A Better Inner Life

When we teach our children to pray, they learn about the joy and peace that are available to them. That joy and peace exceeds anything we can personally offer them, for God, unlike us, is always there to hear and to help. There is the promise of perfect peace (Isaiah 26:3), the joy of God's presence that chases away fear (Psalm 21:6–7), and a reason to have joyful hearts (Psalm 105:3).

When we teach our children to pray, they learn about the joy and peace that are available to them.

Two New Testament writers describe the joy and peace that come through prayer:

> Until now you have not asked for anything in my name. Ask and you will receive, *and your joy will be complete.* (John 16:24, italics added in this and remaining Scriptures for emphasis)

> Do not be anxious about anything, but in everything, by prayer and petition, with thanksgiving, present your requests to God. And *the peace of God, which transcends all understanding, will guard your hearts and your minds in Christ Jesus.* (Philippians 4:6–7, italics added)

2. Personal Growth

All parents desire personal growth for their children. We want our sons and daughters to grow in understanding, wisdom, and the fullness of God. Through prayer, our children can have such growth:

> If you call out for insight and cry aloud for understanding, and if you look for it as for silver and search for it as for hidden treasure, then you will understand the fear of the LORD and find the knowledge of God. *For the LORD gives wisdom,*

and from his mouth come knowledge and understanding.
(Proverbs 2:3–6, italics added)

To know this love that surpasses knowledge—that *you may be filled to the measure of all the fullness of God.* (Ephesians 3:19, italics added; see also Psalm 119:26 and Jeremiah 33:3)

3. Strength and Courage

Our children's fears may seem silly at times, but they are real. And as our children grow into teens and adults, the fears do not go away; they merely change in type. By giving our children the resource of prayer, we provide them with the strength, even courage, to face their world. The Scriptures describe the answers that come through prayer:

I sought the LORD, and he answered me; *he delivered me from all my fears. Those who look to him are radiant; their faces are never covered with shame.* (Psalm 34:4–5, italics added)

When I called, *you answered me; you made me bold and stouthearted.* (Psalm 138:3, italics added; see also 1 Chronicles 16:11, Lamentations 3:57, and Acts 4:31)

4. Protection and Rescue from Harm and Evil

Many issues threaten our children today, ranging from violent crime to drug abuse. There is also the threat of evil influence. Through our prayers and theirs come protection and deliverance from harm's way:

The righteous cry out, and the LORD hears them; *he delivers them from all their troubles.* (Psalm 34:17, italics added; see also Psalm 22:4 and Matthew 6:13)

5. Purpose, Guidance, and Direction for Their Lives

God desires that we and our children call upon Him for guidance and direction in our lives. He has a purpose for each of us, and He promises to fulfill His purpose when we ask:

I cry out to God Most High, to God, *who fulfills his purpose for me.* (Psalm 57:2, italics added; see also Proverbs 3:4–6 and James 1:5)

6. Provision

Our children pray to a loving Father, who has both the desire and power to grant them all that they (and we) need. All they need to do is ask for His provision. As Jesus told His listeners, if a son can rightly expect his earthly father to give him food and good gifts, "how much more will your Father in heaven give good gifts to those who ask him!" (Matthew 7:9–11, italics added).

Here are two New Testament passages that note how our gracious God will give to those who seek after Him:

> So do not worry, saying, "What shall we eat?" or "What shall we drink?" or "What shall we wear?" For the pagans run after all these things, and your heavenly Father knows that you need them. But seek first his kingdom and his righteousness, *and all these things will be given to you as well.* (Matthew 6:31–33, italics added)

> He who did not spare his own Son, but gave him up for us all—how will he not also, along with him, *graciously give us all things*? (Romans 8:32, italics added)

7. Fulfillment of Desires

Another benefit of prayer is that God fulfills our desires. Through prayer and a deepening relationship we learn to delight in Him and He begins to fulfill the desires of our hearts:

> Delight yourself in the LORD and *he will give you the desires of your heart.* (Psalm 37:4, italics added; see also Psalm 21:2 and Proverbs 10:24)

8. Help and Encouragement

Through their prayers, our children can find help and encouragement for their everyday activities. As a Father, God listens, comforts, and sheds grace upon our children as they pray to Him:

> Let us then approach the throne of grace with confidence, so that we may *receive mercy and find grace to help us in our time of need.* (Hebrews 4:16, italics added; see also Psalm 10:17)

9. Promotion and Honor

Finally, God exalts and honors those who honor Him:

> No one from the east or the west or from the desert can exalt a man. But it is God who judges: He brings one down, *he exalts another.* (Psalm 75:6–7, italics added; see also 1 Samuel 2:7)

Humble yourselves before the Lord, and *he will lift you up.* (James 4:10, italics added)

If I said to you, "I have the secret that will help you raise children who are at peace inside, are always growing personally, are courageous, have a strong character, stay out of trouble, and steer clear of evil," would you want to know that secret? If this secret also gave your children a solid sense of direction and purpose—all that they need and then some—and would make them honored and thought highly of by their friends and peers, would you want to know it?

The secret is simple: Teach them to pray.

Made for Prayer

If we go back to the very beginning we see that prayer, communication with God, has always been central. Adam and Eve's relationship with God developed through conversations with Him—through prayer. We know they were accustomed to spending time with God in the garden for they recognized His presence because of a familiar sound and did not show any surprise when He talked to them (Genesis 3:8–10). However, the straightforward, loving communication between God and humankind was short-circuited because of sin, guilt, and each person's desire to seek self. But God created us to communicate with Him.

Humans are engineered for religious faith.

We are designed for prayer. Therefore, even though sin has interfered with the communication channels, the call in our hearts to pray still survives.

Prayer is a concept that every culture and every people throughout time have understood. As far back as historians and archaeologists can find, there is evidence that people had some concept and practice of prayer.[2]

Today, prayer is a hot topic. "Faith and Healing" became the *Time* magazine cover story for the June 24, 1996, issue. The subtitle for the lead article read, "Can prayer, faith and spirituality really improve your physical health? A growing and surprising body of scientific evidence says they can." The article reported the highlights of some of the more than two hundred studies that have been done on the role and effect of religious issues in our lives. Those studies consistently concluded that religious faith, church attendance, and prayer seemed to increase the quality of life.[3] Prayer is everywhere today because it works!

Harvard's Herbert Benson, author of many studies on the effects of religious faith on healing, tells us another reason prayer is so pervasive: We are actually engineered for religious faith. "Humans are . . . wired for God."[4] God created men and women to communicate with and receive from Him. That was the original intent of prayer.

The purpose for creation was to serve people. The purpose for people was to be God's children and to receive His love.

Our Greatest Blessing

Jesus said that the two greatest commandments were to love God and to love others (Matthew 22:37–40). Since we know that God is love and, therefore, completely unselfish, we know that everything He requires of us is for our own good and benefit, not His. Therefore, God's greatest commands must point us toward life's greatest blessings.

The greatest and highest blessing and pleasure that we can have is to have a healthy, growing relationship with God our Father and Creator. The second greatest blessing is to have healthy, growing, loving relationships with others. These are to be the two focal points of our existence, and the keys to our fulfillment. Everything else is sets and props.

Since this is true, and we see all around us the spectacular balance, intricacy, and interdependence of creation, it's easy to conclude that God designed everything else in harmony with these two original objectives or ultimate blessings.

All the studies being done today in the name of science and medical research confirm again and again that this is true. When we function according to God's design, with faith in Him and at peace with others, we are healthier, live longer, and enjoy life.

God, in designing us, designed every part of us and everything around us to be in harmony and absolute agreement with the purpose and blessings for which He created us. It's like the cars we drive. When cars are built, the goal is practical convenience and enjoyable transportation. Everything that is built into cars is put there to serve this purpose and to work in cooperation with every other part. In a similar way, all the natural factors around us, and especially in our own bodies, cooperate with God's design. We pray. We relax. Peace comes.

When we teach our children to pray, we hand them the keys to life. When we don't, they possess a beautiful car designed to take them practically, conveniently, and enjoyably on life's journey, yet they are forced to walk because they don't have the keys.

Like us, our children are designed for prayer. Jesus invites all of us to enter into the greatest blessing we can experience: a relationship with God. In that relationship, all things become possible.

- Prayer reveals God's favor and purpose.
- Prayer demonstrates God's love.
- Prayer offers us access to truth, wisdom, and understanding.
- Prayer lets us enter into real life.
- Prayer brings joy and peace.
- Prayer offers us guidance and direction.
- Prayer gives us strength to resist temptation and to avoid evil.
- Prayer helps us to avoid and/or solve troubles and problems.
- Prayer transforms lives by God's grace at work in hearts.
- Through prayer, we receive answers to everyday requests.
- Through prayer, miracles become possible.
- Through prayer, the desires of our hearts are granted.

Prayer Is Not the Goal

Now, in case you're wondering, I am not saying that prayer is an end in itself or something that we just add into the mix of our children's lives to give them yet another advantage among advantages. In fact, I'm saying the opposite. Prayer is not an addition to their lives. Prayer is part of the very foundation of their lives. It is one of the most important things our children need to learn.

Also, the long list of advantages we've considered doesn't just happen because we teach our children to spend a certain amount of time on their knees repeating prayers or giving God today's shopping list. Although extended time and multiple requests sometimes are part of our prayers, those times in themselves are not prayer. Teaching our children to pray is teaching them to communicate and grow in a relationship with God as they seek Him and His will. It's a life of prayer or growing with God that yields these benefits.

Prayer is not an end in itself. Nor should it be a way of merely accessing these benefits. Prayer is the gateway to God's love.

Questions

1. List five ways you can give prayer a more central role in your family's life.

_____

_____

_____

_____

_____

2. What are some things—such as a busy schedule, misplaced priorities, or financial concerns—that get in the way of your family's prayer life?

_____

_____

_____

Take time to set these things before God in prayer and ask Him to help you incorporate more time for prayer into your family's daily and weekly routine.

Ideas for Prayer

- Thank God for the joy of spending time with Him in prayer.
- Ask God to help you give your children the best, in everything.
- Ask God to help you make spiritual teaching and training a priority in your home.

Prayer for Kids

Here is a sample prayer your children could pray.

"Thank You, Lord, that You want to be my heavenly Father and take care of me and show me how to be wise. Please help me to do things Your way. Also, please help me learn how to pray. In Jesus' name, amen."

---

1. "The Parenting Poll," *Parenting,* December/January 1996, 123.
2. Plutarch, the Greek biographer and historian who lived almost two thousand years ago, said, "If we traverse the world, it is possible to find cities without walls, without letters, without wealth, without coin, without schools or theaters: but a city without a temple, or that practices not worship, prayers and the like, no one has ever seen." C. L. Sulzberger, *Go Gentle into the Good Night* (Englewood Cliffs, N. J.: Prentice-Hall, 1976), 24.
3. Claudia Wallis, "Faith & Healing," *Time,* 24 June 1996.
4. Quoted in Wallis, *Time,* 24 June 1996, 61.

CHAPTER 2

Prayer Is for Kids

Prayer Is for Kids

Since my youth, O God, you have taught me, and to this day I declare your marvelous deeds. Even when I am old and gray, do not forsake me, O God, till I declare your power to the next generation, your might to all who are to come.

(Psalm 71:17–18)

Jesus came that we might know God's love and see it in action. He showed us what was close to God's heart.

What Jesus Said About Children

When we try to think about a time Jesus got upset, one picture probably comes to mind: Jesus cleaning out the temple with His whip made of cords (John 2:14–16). The next picture to come to our minds might be of Jesus blasting the religious leaders for their hypocrisy and blindness. But the Bible records another time when Jesus became indignant. His anger concerned the treatment of children. When recounting Jesus' words, we often emphasize that Jesus was telling us adults that we need to receive the kingdom of God like a little child. That is a valid point, but it's not the main one Jesus was making here:

> People were bringing little children to Jesus to have him touch them, but the disciples rebuked them. When Jesus

saw this, he was indignant. He said to them, "Let the little children come to me, and do not hinder them, for the kingdom of God belongs to such as these. I tell you the truth, anyone who will not receive the kingdom of God like a little child will never enter it." And he took the children in his arms, put his hands on them and blessed them. (Mark 10:13–16)

God created people to have a relationship with Him from childhood.

Jesus and His disciples were out preaching and teaching about the kingdom of God. While they were doing so, some people tried to bring children to Jesus to have Him bless them. The disciples rebuked them, probably with words such as, "Can't you see the Master is busy? He's doing important work teaching adults. He doesn't have time for children." Jesus saw the commotion and was indignant. He probably was indignant not just at the disciples' rebuke but at the attitudes and ideas that led to it.

Welcoming Little Children

God doesn't shun children (see Mark 10:14) nor wait until they are older, wiser, or more important. He created people to have a relationship with Him from childhood.

A commonly reported Gallup poll found that 85 percent of people who give their lives to Christ make the decision to do so before age eighteen. Dr. James Dobson, a well-known psychologist, author, and host of the nationally syndicated radio show *Focus on the Family*, writes, "There is a brief period during childhood when youngsters are vulnerable to religious training. Their concepts of right and wrong . . . are formulated during this time, and their view of God begins to solidify."[1] The Bible says, "Train a child in the way he should go, and when he is old he will not turn from it" (Proverbs 22:6).

Jesus knew that when God created us, He made us to know Him and learn from Him. This begins the day we are born. Jesus basically said to the disciples, "We're out here telling people about the kingdom of God. When the ideal candidates for learning come forward, you try to keep them away. Don't!" He drove home His point by saying, "I tell you the truth, anyone who will not receive the kingdom of God like a little child will never enter it" (verse 15). Children are so much the perfect candidates for God's kingdom that unless the adults become like them again they can't enter it.

Jesus knew that since people were made to learn about and embrace Him as children, taking kids in the opposite direction during this vulnerable time would affect them negatively. How did He feel about those who did that? Look at the language Jesus used to demonstrate His heart in Matthew 18:5-6. Gordon Dalbey, in his book *Fight Like a Man*, puts it perfectly: "Indeed, Jesus reserved his most fierce lashing for those who undermine a child's faith in him; they're not just to be tossed overboard for a slap on the wrist, but weighted down; not just with something heavy, but 'a large millstone'; not just in the hands, 'but around his neck'; not just in the shallows, but 'the deep sea.'"[2]

Another time Jesus talked about children:

They came to Capernaum. When he was in the house, he asked them, "What were you arguing about on the road?" But they kept quiet because on the way they had argued about who was the greatest. Sitting down, Jesus called the Twelve and said, "If anyone wants to be first, he must be the very last, and the servant of all."

He took a little child and had him stand among them. Taking him in his arms, he said to them, "Whoever welcomes one of these little children in my name welcomes me; and whoever welcomes me does not welcome me but the one who sent me." (Mark 9:33–37)

After telling His disciples that the key to being first, or greatest, is to be the servant of all, Jesus took a child in His arms and said, "If you welcome one of these little children, you are directly serving God." Jesus simply said, not only for the sake of example, but because He meant it, "If you want to be the greatest in my kingdom, welcome (serve, teach, love, call, spend time with) children!"

Jesus' service to children was comprehensive. He blessed and prayed for children. He called His disciples to serve them. He had children help Him at least once by contributing a lunch. The Bible records that children were in His audiences, listening to His teaching. Jesus healed them, raised them from the dead, took them in His arms, and welcomed them into His kingdom. He called us to do the same. He went to great lengths to impress the importance of children on His followers.

Reflections

Read Deuteronomy 6:6–9. How can you apply this passage to your family's prayer life? To each of your children's? For example, how could you work a lesson about God's faithfulness into an everyday activity like grocery shopping or studying for a test?

_____

_____

_____

Learning from Jesus' Childhood

The term *personal relationship*, when applied to our relationship with God, has come to mean that a person has accepted Jesus' work on the cross and has become a Christian. In fact, at that point a person has merely received a formal introduction to God. A personal relationship is, or should be, the goal and pursuit of life beyond this introduction. The primary method of that pursuit is, of course, prayer.

Let's look at the example Jesus set, and especially at what we know of His childhood, to see the example He set for our children.

A Child's Wisdom

When Jesus was twelve years old, His parents took Him to Jerusalem for the Feast of the Passover "according to the custom. After the Feast was over, while his parents were returning home, the boy Jesus stayed behind in Jerusalem, but they were unaware of it." When Mary and Joseph realized their son was missing, they returned to search for Him. Within three days they found Him "in the temple courts, sitting among the teachers, listening to them and asking them questions. Everyone who heard him was amazed at his understanding and his answers" (Luke 2:42–43, 46–47).

Jesus' parents found Him after three days, sitting among the teachers. What took place during those three days? During the Feast of the Passover, the temple would have been full of visitors from all over the Roman Empire. Many would have been interested in seeking greater understanding of the Scriptures from the teachers. The teachers would have gathered to expound their beliefs and understanding of God's Word to appreciative audiences. They would not have gathered together merely to talk with and listen to a twelve-year-old! So it's safe to assume that what Jesus' parents witnessed on the third day was the culmination of a series of events. Jesus' understanding and answers were seemingly so astounding that, slowly but surely over the course of three days, He won the audience. His audience was not just some of the teachers—the text says "the teachers," implying *all* of them. Jesus had apparently won the interest of all the teachers gathered, and probably of those who came to listen to them.

Even a child, when spending time with God and learning from Him, can confound people who, by the world's standards, are wise and well educated. The Bible says, "For the foolishness of God is wiser than man's wisdom, and the weakness of God is stronger than man's strength" (1 Corinthians 1:25). When our children start spending time with God, we (and others) will notice the difference.

> **When our children start spending time with God, we (and others) will notice the difference.**

Here's what Jesus said as an adult. (I wonder if He was reflecting back on His three days in the temple?) "I praise you, Father, Lord of heaven and earth, because you have hidden these things from the wise and learned, and revealed them to little children. Yes, Father, for this was your good pleasure" (Luke 10:21).

Learning As Children Learn

The book of Proverbs says that the fear of the Lord is the beginning of wisdom. Children don't look at their own intelligence and discernment as the source of all wisdom. As adults, however, we tend to trust ourselves to decide what is right, and we end up thinking we *are* right. But God designed us to learn from Him as children and to build on what we learn by continuing to learn as adults. When, as children, we aren't taught to learn from God, it's easy to get stuck on what we did learn and to stop growing. How wonderful to have the opportunity to direct our children to learn from God now and prepare the way for them to keep learning throughout their lives!

> **God designed us to learn from Him as children and to build on what we learn by continuing to learn as adults.**

If we look at the two progress reports given about Jesus' childhood that sandwich the story of His visit to the temple, we'll see that although Jesus was God's Son, it was His Father's plan that He learn about God and grow in relationship with Him, as children were meant to. He learned about and from God, not as part of the Godhead, but as a child born in relationship with Him: "And the child grew and became strong; he was filled with wisdom, and the grace of God was upon him. . . . And Jesus grew in wisdom and stature, and in favor with God and men" (Luke 2:40, 52). From this we can conclude the following about Jesus' childhood and spiritual development:

- Jesus grew in wisdom, or mentally, which was achieved according to God's purpose through His Jewish education, His parents' teaching, and His study of the Torah.
- Jesus grew in stature, or physically, which was accomplished by natural growth and food consumption.
- Jesus grew in favor with God, or spiritually, through submission to Him and His will, and through prayer.
- Jesus grew in favor with men, or socially, which was accomplished through being involved in His neighborhood, community, and synagogue, and learning through serving and loving others.

Jesus didn't come into this world merely quoting Scripture and talking with God as He had for eternity prior. He became in every way like us, so He could identify with us and we could identify with Him. This gave Him the ability to become like us in being tempted and in suffering (see Hebrews 2:17–18; 5:8–9). Just like every other child, Jesus grew, learned, and obeyed His parents according to God's perfect plan.

Now, we know that "Christian" means "Christlike," and as adult Christians we know that we are to follow Christ's example in regard to attitude, service, commitment to God, and so on. But who are Christian children to identify with? With the Jesus who is recorded in Luke 2! He was in their shoes and set the example for them to follow.

Jesus started as a child and grew up with God as His Guide, His Father, His Teacher, His Friend. He grew up the way God meant for children to grow up—in an awesome relationship with their Father and Creator. Jesus facilitated His incredible relationship with the Father as our children can, through study of the Scriptures, submission to God's will, and, primarily, through growth in prayer.

Jesus was the first child to grow up on earth the way God intended—the way Cain and Abel would have if their parents hadn't chosen to go their own way. Who Jesus was, and became, was as much because of that as any other factor. Jesus would not have had to learn a thing from anyone, except that it was God's design that He do so for our sakes. That's why, when God chose Abraham long before, He chose him and prepared him *so that* he would bring his children up to follow God (Genesis 18:19). A vital part of God's plan was that, when Jesus came, His parents would know how to raise Him and train Him.

Learning from Jesus' Godly Parents

Many of us give little thought to the parenting skills and dedication of Mary and Joseph. We sometimes think that having Jesus as a son must have been a breeze. They just fed Him and He grew up to be an awesome prophet. Wrong! That could have happened if God had wanted it, but He had planned something else for our benefit.

Mary and Joseph had an awesome privilege and responsibility to fulfill all of God's commands about bringing up their child in the way He should go. God selected and prepared them, as He had selected Abraham and Sarah much earlier, so that they would bring up God's Son in the way God meant for children to be raised.

Mary was visited by an angel who told her that she was going to get pregnant out of wedlock. Women of that time were stoned for that. Yet, "'I am the Lord's servant,' Mary answered. 'May it be to me as you have said.' Then the angel left her" (Luke 1:38). Later, when Mary visited Elizabeth, her song was full of language and quotes from the Old Testament: She knew her Bible (Luke 1:45–55)!

Joseph accepted God's command to take Mary, pregnant but not with his child, as his wife. Joseph accepted the responsibility of adopting and calling God's Son his own.

The presence of prayer in our children's lives is the presence of the person and power of God.

Mary and Joseph followed God's leading, moving their family all over the place. In every recorded event about Jesus' parents, the Bible shows that they were doing their best to follow and please God. They were devout and committed followers of God and were chosen to raise God's only Son the way children were meant to be raised: in partnership with God. And that is what they did.

Jesus is pictured in the accounts of His ministry as being a man of prayer. He said that His every action and word were the Father's and were guided by prayer. He went away to pray regularly, and His relationship with God was His most prized possession. Although Jesus has always had a relationship with God as part of the Godhead, as a human for our benefit He developed a relationship with God on earth that began in His childhood.

We too can teach our children to pray so they can develop a relationship with God according to the example that has been set. That is how we can prepare them to be everything God made them to be, to learn everything God wants them to know, and to receive every blessing their loving heavenly Father has for them. The presence of prayer in our children's lives is the presence of the person and power of God.

Now, in case you're having visions of your children spending all their time on their knees, becoming fanatics or being a little weird, remember that Jesus was a regular boy. He fit into the community. The verse we looked at earlier said that He grew in favor with God and men. He was probably a carpenter's apprentice. He worked, He ate, He slept. He was part of a regular family and grew up living life as all children do.

By Mary and Joseph agreeing to raise Jesus, God's Son, the way they were instructed to raise Him, they paved the way for God to put parenting right again. God, once again through Jesus' work, will assist us in raising our children, just like He had planned to do before Adam and Eve fell. Mary and Joseph, through their obedience, trust, and raising Jesus in faith and partnership with God, opened the way for every parent and child who would accept Jesus to return to God's original and awesome plan.

God is ready, willing, and able to move into your home today, take your children in His arms, and begin teaching them, caring for them, and drawing them to Himself. He also is ready to work in us and give us the wisdom, love, strength, and everyday practical ability to do our part in the process. We don't work from the foundation of being perfect now or getting it all exactly right, but from the foundation of God's love, grace, and faithfulness.

We also can become like little children; we can put aside our pride and ask God to teach us, change us, help us, and cause us to do what is right. We can receive His wisdom, love, care, and intervention on a daily basis. We, as parents, are not left alone.

God loves our children. He has fought and won the greatest custody battle in history! He has opened the way for all children to come back into His love and plan again. A child who learns how to pray and begins to grow in relationship with God will really discover life, every part of it, the way God created it to be—a full, abundant life. As Jesus declared, "I have come that they may have life, and have it to the full" (John 10:10).

Learning to Trust God's Care

Ironically, many prayers are not answered simply because we do not trust enough to ask. "You do not have, because you do not ask God," the apostle James declared bluntly (4:2).

The reason we don't have what we want in our lives, the apostle wrote, is because we don't pray. And when we do pray, "You do not receive, because you ask with wrong motives, that you may spend what you get on your pleasures" (verse 3). In other words, we are sure we know what is best for us. So we basically pray for our will to be done. "This is what I want and this is how I want it."

James was not saying that we can't get the things we need and want by praying; nor was he saying that we should pray only for things for others. What he was saying is that in effective prayer we put ourselves in God's care. Prayer is the means by which we communicate with God, develop a relationship with Him, and learn to trust Him. God wants us to trust Him, to seek Him, His wisdom, His plans for us, and His best.

Trusting in God's Love

God is love. Love is unselfish. Therefore, everything God requires of us or has for us is for our benefit. When we are calling the shots and demanding our own way, it's probably because we haven't realized the awesome privilege and opportunity of prayer and relationship with God. It's like going to the world's greatest financial counselor, handing him our money and an exact list of what we want him to do with it, and then walking out without getting so much as an opinion from him about our plan.

Prayer is submitting ourselves to and seeking God's will, trusting that His will for us is very good.

Later in his epistle James wrote, "Humble yourselves before the Lord, and he will lift you up" (4:10).

By "humble yourselves," he meant stop thinking that you know best; stop wanting it your way; submit yourself to His love, care, wisdom, principles, and growth process because you know He loves you. Let Him lift you up. Let Him bless you, care for you, give you what you need, and transform you into all that you can be and all that He created you to be.

Prayer is submitting ourselves to and seeking God's will, trusting that His will for us is very good.

The Bible says some pretty phenomenal things about what God wants for us and our children and about what He is not only willing to do but wants to do, as we pray and trust Him with our lives and teach our children to do likewise. In Jeremiah 29:11–13, God declares:

> "For I know the plans I have for you," declares the LORD, "plans to prosper you and not to harm you, plans to give you hope and a future. Then you will call upon me and come and pray to me, and I will listen to you. You will seek me and find me when you seek me with all your heart."

(See Psalm 40:5, 86:5; and Ephesians 3:20 for other declarations of God's good plans for our lives and His power to fulfill them.)

Answered Prayer: Part of Growing in Relationship with Him

God wants to do all these wonderful things in our children's lives as they grow physically and spiritually. He also made it pretty clear that, as we submit to His love and will, we can count on Him to respond to our specific requests and prayers and to demonstrate His love in our lives. But read closely. It's always in the context of our growing in relationship with Him and, ultimately, trusting His love.

> If you remain in me and my words remain in you, ask whatever you wish, and it will be given you. (John 15:7; see also John 14:13–14; 15:16; 16:23–24)

> Dear friends, if our hearts do not condemn us, we have confidence before God and receive from him anything we ask, because we obey his commands and do what pleases him. And this is his command: to believe in the name of his Son, Jesus Christ, and to love one another as he commanded us. (1 John 3:21–23)

> This is the confidence we have in approaching God: that if we ask anything according to his will, he hears us. And if we know that he hears us—whatever we ask—we know that we have what we asked of him. (1 John 5:14–15)

In this last verse, John was saying the same thing as James: We'll receive our answer if we ask, not according to our will but according to His will. How do we pray according to God's will? By acknowledging two principles.

First, the Bible is God's revealed will. Therefore we know that praying for things outside of what the Bible says God will do, or asking God to do something contrary to who He is, opposes God's will. For example, the Bible says, "God is love," and God requires us to love others. Therefore praying for God to "get" someone we don't like won't work. Beyond that, praying according to God's will is the trusting attitude with which we pray, more than the specific things we ask for. Consider these two prayers about the same thing. Which is the more trusting?

"God, my car broke down and I need a new one. Please get my loan approved."

"God, as You already know, my car broke down today. Please give me Your wisdom and help me know what to do."

Second, God's will for us is good. Prayer in its many forms composes the communication aspect of our relationship with God. In our prayers we place our lives—everything we think, do, and are concerned about—into His loving arms. Then we trust Him to teach us and train us, provide for us, and protect us. We trust Him to show us what we were made to do, guide us to be the best we can be, help us live the best life we can live, and have the best relationship possible with Him, our loving and faithful God: our Father.

God's Love

Most of the strongest Bible passages written about God giving us anything we ask for in prayer were written by the disciple John, who described himself as "the disciple whom Jesus loved" (John 21:7, 20). Now I'm sure John did not think the other eleven weren't loved or were loved less. Rather, he saw in Jesus just how much God loved him and how much He loves us all. Because John knew how much he was loved, he had no trouble believing that God would answer his prayers.

This is what we want our children to know: that God loves them.

When we start to teach our children to pray, they won't begin as prayer giants. A close relationship with God needs to be developed. We can't force this relationship. We can only direct, teach, and encourage it. The key to teaching our children to pray is to help them understand and get to know who God is and, little by little by calling attention to answered prayer, to help them see God's love for them. As they see God's love demonstrated for them, we can encourage them to put their whole lives—each concern, event, and desire—into His trust-worthy, loving care. The more our children see of God's love and character, the more their trust and faith in Him will grow. And like John, when they can truly realize how much God loves them, they'll experience His power, care, wisdom, and love daily. Effective prayer comes through a growing relationship with God.

Reflections

1. What are some areas of life which you have difficulty turning over to God? Finances? Work? Your marriage? Take a few minutes to write them down.

   _____

   _____

   _____

2. What steps can you take to help yourself trust God more in these areas?

   _____

   _____

   _____

3. Name two ways you can use your struggles with each of these issues to teach your children about prayer.

   _____

   _____

   _____

4. List three things that can help you discover God's will in these areas. How can you teach these things to your children?

_____

_____

_____

5. Describe three ways you can assure your children of God's love for them.

_____

_____

_____

A Child's Faith

An excellent example of how effective prayer comes through relationship with God is the boy we met at the beginning of this section, George Washington Carver. George lived from 1864 to 1943. He was born a slave, and after his mom and dad were killed, he was raised by his master. Several years after the Emancipation Proclamation was signed, George, then age ten or twelve, left home to go to school. His life of faith included his belief in the power of prayer.

George graduated from high school in 1885. From there he went on to receive a bachelor's degree in agricultural science in 1894 and a master of science degree in 1896 from Iowa State Agricultural College. He was the first black both to graduate from the college and to serve on the faculty. He then accepted an invitation to head the Department of Agriculture at the Tuskegee Institute in Alabama.

Amid the depleted farmland of the South, devastated by years of planting and harvesting only one crop, cotton, Carver introduced peanuts and sweet potatoes. He found that the two new crops not only grew well in the devastated soil, they restored it!

The farmers succeeded so well with their peanuts and sweet

potatoes that they couldn't find enough markets for their crops. As was Carver's custom, he took the problem to God. He said God showed him to take the peanut apart. After much laboratory research, George ultimately developed three hundred derivative products from peanuts and, using the same process, one hundred eighteen from sweet potatoes. Among these products were plastics, medicinal oils, ink, dyes, instant "coffee," linoleum, cosmetics, flour, cheese, powdered milk, wood stains, synthetic rubber, vinegar, molasses, postage stamp glue, fertilizer, and many more.

George Washington Carver said that before each set of experiments he would go to the Creator and ask Him what he should do. He said, "My discoveries come like a divine revelation from God. The idea and the method of working out a new product come all together. . . ."[3]

As a result of Carver's work, agriculture and, therefore the economy of the South, was renewed. Before his work, the peanut was not even considered a crop. By the 1940s, it was the second largest cash crop in the South.

Carver's lifetime list of achievements goes on and on. His fame spread all over the world. Foreign governments asked for his counsel. Henry Ford worked closely with him. Presidents Calvin Coolidge and Franklin D. Roosevelt came and met with him. He was given many prestigious awards and honors. Thomas A. Edison, among many others, offered him more than $100,000 a year to come and work for him. Carver declined and never left the Tuskegee Institute because he felt that God wanted him where he was.

"A personal relationship with the great Creator of all things is the only foundation for the abundant life"

In 1944 Congress passed a law setting aside January 5th as George Washington Carver Day. In 1953 they authorized a National Monument in his honor at the site of the farm where he was raised, which was also the place where he first learned to simply talk to and trust his Father by asking Him for a knife.

George Washington Carver said in a public address: "A personal relationship with the great Creator of all things is the only foundation for the abundant life. Walk and talk with God and let Him direct your path. Some people never really touch life because they are bound up in themselves. . . . You must get in touch with the Creator if you want to be lifted above the little things of life."[4]

Activity: Make a Faith Stories Book

1. Make a Faith Stories book or prayer journal with your children. There are two ways you can do this. First, you could buy a book with blank pages and decorate the cover with pictures cut out from magazines or ones your children draw. Then draw lines on the pages to divide them into spaces where your children can record the date, a brief description of what they are praying for, and the answer with its own date. You can leave space for the answer below the prayer (as below) or beside it.

Date: _____ My Prayer: _____

_____

_____

Date: _____ God's Answer: _____

_____

_____

Second, you could make your own book using colored or personally decorated paper. Fold the papers into the size you want the book to be. Join the papers together like a book with thick staples or by sewing them with thick thread or thin string. If necessary, carefully cut the edges of the folded papers so that they can open. Then divide each page with lines into the spaces as in number 1, above.

2. After making your child's personal Faith Stories book, write his or her first prayer in it together. Each night as you put your child to bed you can add prayers or reread the ones there and, when God answers, write the answer and the date in the

space beside the prayer. Soon your child will have a record of God's faithfulness to him or her to treasure for years—a solid reminder of God's love and care.

Questions

1. When was the last time you received a specific answer to prayer?

_____

_____

_____

Make a list of prayers God has answered for you lately and share them with your children. This will help to encourage them that God will answer their prayers. Have them make a list of some of the things they've prayed about.

_____

_____

_____

2. What new ideas about children and prayer did you learn in this chapter?

_____

_____

_____

3. How has your attitude toward children and prayer affected the way you teach your children about prayer?

_____

_____

_____

4. What elements of Mary and Joseph's lives can you apply to your own life as a parent? How?

    _____

    _____

    _____

5. There are some elements in the story of Jesus as a child in the temple (Luke 2:41–52) that your children can understand and relate to their own experiences. The discussion questions following the story will help you pull out and discuss aspects of the story that your children can identify with.

    Every year Jesus' parents went to Jerusalem for the Passover Feast. When he was 12 years old, they went up to the Feast as usual.

    After the Feast was over, his parents left to go back home. The boy Jesus stayed behind in Jerusalem. But they were not aware of it. They thought he was somewhere in their group. So they traveled on for a day.

    Then they began to look for him among their relatives and friends. They did not find him. So they went back to Jerusalem to look for him. After three days they found him in the temple courtyard. He was sitting with the teachers. He was listening to them and asking them questions. Everyone who heard him was amazed at how much he understood. They also were amazed at his answers.

    When his parents saw him, they were amazed. His mother said to him, "Son, why have you treated us like this? Your father and I have been worried about you. We have been looking for you everywhere."

    "Why were you looking for me?" he asked. "Didn't you know I had to be in my Father's house?" But they did not understand what he meant by that.

    Then he went back to Nazareth with them, and he obeyed them. But his mother kept all these things like a secret treasure in her heart. Jesus became wiser and stronger. He also became more and more pleasing to God and to people. (NIrV)

- How do you think Jesus felt about going on the trip?
- Are there ever times when you have to go somewhere with your parents, even if you don't want to?
- How do you think Jesus' parents felt when they found out He was not with them?
- Have you ever been lost? How did it feel?
- What did the teachers and other people at the temple think of Jesus?
- Do you think Jesus was too young to be asking about God? Why or why not?
- Why did Jesus tell His mother He was in His Father's house?
- It doesn't seem that Jesus' parents understood Him at this point. Can you think of a time when you thought your parents didn't understand you? How did that feel?
- Why do you think Jesus became wiser and more pleasing to God and people?
- What can you do to become wiser and more pleasing to God and people?

Ideas for Prayer
- Thank God for giving you the privilege of teaching your children about Him.
- Ask God to help you keep your life and prayers simple.
- Ask God to help you be a good example to your children.
- Thank God for listening to your prayers.
- Think about some things that your children have trouble trusting God for. Ask God to give them more faith in these areas.
- Take a moment to think about some things that you have difficulty trusting God for. Write them down in the spaces below, then pray and commit them to God. Acknowledge your trust in Him and thank Him for His provision.

_____

_____

_____

Prayer for Kids

Here are some sample prayers your children could pray.

"Dear Father, thank You for wanting me to talk to You. Thank You that I can always trust You. Please help me never to forget this. Father, I'm thinking about _____ and _____. Please take care of these things/people for me. Thank You that I can always turn to You for help. In Jesus' name, amen."

"Dear Father God, I'm so glad You want to talk to me. It is great to be able to tell You what I feel and what I care about. Please help me to pray like Jesus did when He was little. In Jesus' name, amen."

---

1. James Dobson, *Dr. Dobson Answers Your Questions* (Wheaton, Ill.: Tyndale, 1982), 35.
2. Gordon Dalbey, *Fight Like a Man* (Wheaton, Ill.: Tyndale, 1995), 205.
3. From various addresses by Carver, quoted in B. Miller's *George Washington Carver, God's Ebony Scientist* (Grand Rapids: Zondervan, 1943).
4. Ibid.

PART 2

"Get Set"

Still young, but now fully grown, the boy stood 6 feet 4 inches tall. He was thin and gangly, as boys often are when they grow tall so quickly that their motor skills lag behind. Yet he also was big boned and very strong from all the heavy farm work he had been doing since he was old enough to pick up a tool of any sort. He appeared somewhat homely, with severe features topped with dark hair that seemed to do what it pleased. Despite his somber appearance, his quick wit and people-loving personality made him likable and put people at ease.

The youth worked more than he went to school, but he did learn the basics. Only a handful of books were available to him as a boy, among them the Bible and *The Pilgrim's Progress*. Like Pilgrim, the main character in *The Pilgrim's Progress*, his life would bring him face-to-face with the Giant of Despair and take him through Doubting Castle and the Slough of Despond. In fact, his life appeared to have more tragedy and disappointments than victories.

For most of his adult years, prayer was something he did when there was nothing else he could do. But his faith, diligence, honesty, perseverance, and those prayers during difficult times led him up to, and set the stage for, his moments in history. Before he did the things that history records as great, the pressures of one of the world's most difficult responsibilities, combined with having to lead others through life's greatest horror, drove him to realize that without prayer nothing could be accomplished. Abraham Lincoln, the sixteenth president of the United States and commander-in-chief during America's painful Civil War, regarded prayer as his constant foundation.

Although the defining moments of this man's life would help determine who we are as a society, those moments needed to be defined in and through prayer. We will explore Lincoln's faith in prayer further at the end of this section.

Let's now see how we can "get set" to help our children pray.

This section deals with the approach we use to teach our children to pray. In the next section we'll cover the nitty-gritty of prayer, everything from types of prayer, to positions in prayer, to how God answers prayer. But this section is probably the most important in this book because, as we will see, our approach to teaching will largely determine the outcome of that teaching.

Saying Prayers–or Praying?

Saying Prayers– or Praying?

There is a vast difference between saying prayers and praying.

Anonymous

All of us parents are teachers. Our children observe us, imitate us, and learn from us. Our approach to teaching will largely determine the outcome of that teaching. How do we determine our approach? It comes out of our understanding of the basic concepts that undergird our teaching.

How Understanding Affects Our Approach

In short: Who we are, what we believe, and how we understand life to work will affect how we approach teaching our children to pray (among other things), and that approach will determine the outcome.

Our Understanding of Childhood

One example of how understanding affects our approach concerns childhood play. Most parents believe children need a balance between childhood play and growing responsibilities. So we try to give them both. Sometimes we tell our children, "Enjoy your child-hood while it lasts," implying that childhood is supposed to be fun and free from worry and responsibility. At the same time, however, we are implying that adulthood is burdened down with respon-sibilities, worries, and problems. When we accept this as fact, understanding reality to be like this, and act from it in our parent-ing approach, we will get corresponding results and can raise kids who don't want to grow up, who dislike responsibility, and who, as adults, just want to party.

I believe God meant for people to enjoy both childhood and adulthood. He intends that children learn responsibility while young and progressively take on more as they are able to incor-porate it into their lives. Childhood is not to be all fun and games, nor all work, training, and drudgery. It is meant to be a time of progressive training and learning—learning the balance of a godly, responsible, yet fun-filled and wonderful life. And that process has no end. It continues all our lives.

Impact on Teaching Our Children to Pray
If we adopt this philosophy, our approach in teaching prayer takes on a balance. We won't say, "Let them have their child-hood. They'll learn how to pray when they are older." We also won't try to turn our children into perfect little prayer robots who can say all the right things with their eyes closed. Neither achieves the balance God desires for us.

Children who are left to learn prayer when they are older can have great difficulty in turning their lives godward. But those who have the rigors and discipline of a regimented and "must-be-just-so" prayer life pushed on them may lose the connection between their hearts and their prayer life.

The process of prayer comes naturally to children. Again, they are designed to pray. Their prayers grow progressively as they grow with God. Just as any relationship is progressive and continuous-ly growing, so is their relationship with God. When we under-stand this, our approach becomes balanced and incremental.

Understanding God's Assurances for Relationship
As we consider how we approach teaching our children, we should also address a conundrum, a puzzle that presents itself:

Can we teach our children to have a close relationship with God? After all, relationship is a heart issue and cannot be summed up with formulas and principles alone.

Also, there is another partner in this relationship: God, who has His specific will, timing, and calling. Can we make our children love God? Can we make God respond to our children the way we would like Him to? If we have this kind of ambiguity in our hearts, it will surface in our approach and undermine our efforts.

No, we can't ultimately control our children's wills and decisions, and we certainly can't tell God when to do what. However, God has given us some assurances concerning His desire for relationship with children and our role in aiding that relationship. Here are four:

1. *Ongoing relationship.* As we discussed in part 1, it is absolutely central to our children's lives for God to have a growing relationship with them. Indeed, such a relationship is part of God's desire and design.

> **If we have ambiguity in our hearts, it will surface in our approach and undermine our efforts.**

2. *Parents in partnership.* God created parents and placed them in the process for facilitating physical, social, intellectual, and spiritual growth in their children. He gave us this task not to do by ourselves or in our own wisdom but to accomplish in partnership with Him. We can conclude then that God is eager to stand with us in this foundational task and will open wide His end of the communication channel.

3. *Imprinted for growth.* God has established, in His design of children and the growth process, that progressive growth in Him builds strength. Also, progressive growth in Him from childhood creates an imprint that matches the very essence of who we are and how we were created. Solomon said in the book of Proverbs, "Train a child in the way he should go, and when he is old he will not turn from it" (Proverbs 22:6). Therefore, we can take comfort that with each step in the process, God

is working in our children and drawing them closer to Himself. And He has imprinted our children with the natural ability to respond and grow.

4. *The Scriptures as a resource.* We also know that God gives principles, tips, and guidance for learning to pray and developing a relationship with Him in the Bible, just as He does for other relationships, like marriage. God doesn't play games with us. When He gives principles and instructions to help us or our children to know Him, He gives them because He plans to respond. He desires to work with us as parents.

If we understand with our minds and hearts these four principles, our approach in teaching prayer will reflect it. When we know that the process and outcome are God's will and design and that He is working with us to achieve that end, our faith increases and peace comes. As parents, we will be like world-class coaches who have confidence in a great outcome, knowing the young athlete has the potential, and we, the coaches, have all the resources we need. Our confidence in the process, which comes from understanding that the process is God's will and design, brings patience, faith, wonder, and joy to our approach. This approach will facilitate the natural and successful outcome: children who love God, know Him, and hold that relationship as the foundation for everything else in their lives. In other words, it will produce children who know how to pray.

All of life will become the platform for teaching prayer.

Remembering Prayer as Communication

Another way our understanding affects our approach and its results is found in our understanding of the nature of prayer. Remember, (1) prayer is the communication element of our relationship with God, and (2) a relationship with God is to be the foundation of our lives. When we understand these two truths, our approach with our children will reflect that. All of life will become the platform for teaching prayer, not just bedtime, mealtime, and trouble time. Having relationship with God as the goal will take the number one focus away from obtaining things and receiving quick fixes.

Sincere prayer and honest conversation with God become more important in the teaching process than just doing that prayer thing we do each night so we can say we did it. Also, personal growth in Christ becomes a natural by-product of prayer because part of our relationship with God is receiving His wisdom and accepting His teaching, guidance, and correction.

The rest of this section will cover some key principles of approach that will help you get the job done and help you and your children enjoy the process.

Questions

1. What's the relationship between "understanding," "approach," and "results" when it comes to teaching your children about prayer?

   _____

   _____

   _____

2. Where do you find you struggle most in teaching your children how to pray, in your understanding or your approach? Why?

   _____

   _____

   _____

   How might you change this?

   _____

   _____

   _____

3. What are some ways that your approach to teaching your children to pray has suffered because of your lack of understanding about prayer?

_____

_____

_____

Ideas for Prayer
- Thank God for all that He is teaching you about prayer.
- Ask God to inspire you with creative ideas for teaching your children about prayer.

Prayer for Kids
Here is a sample prayer your children could use.

"Dear Father God, thanks for listening to me. Please help me to know You better. Thank You for loving me and being my friend. In Jesus' name, amen."

KISS: Keep It Simple and Sincere

PRAYER LESSONS

INTERCESSOR - Someone who prays during recess.

PETITION - A paper everyone signs when we all want God to do something.

TRESPASS - something my dad says bad drivers do

KISS: Keep It Simple and Sincere

A man prayed, and at first he thought that prayer was talking. But he became more and more quiet until in the end he realized that prayer is listening.

Søren Kierkegaard

When I was eighteen years old, I accepted the fact that Jesus died for me. I asked God to forgive me and take control of my life. My decision was so life-changing that I was off like a shot, trying to get to know God better and learn everything there was to know about Him and the Bible. I attended every church service, Bible study, and prayer meeting I could find. I attended meetings five, even six nights a week, plus two services on Sunday.

During this time, I learned to love the concept of prayer. I had learned to pray as a child and remembered talking to God in my own words or crying to Him when I was upset or troubled. But this was new and different. I listened intently every time someone prayed. I asked questions and read books. After a while, I became what I thought was an expert at praying. I would pray in public meetings, reciting the exact prayer formulas I had heard from others. I had one for each occasion and problem.

When I was alone, sometimes I'd pray nonstop for one to two hours. I thought I knew the correct prayers to pray and the correct Scriptures to quote for any event—for people in any circumstance, for church services and meetings, for weddings, for family occasions. I had prayers for bedtime and for the morning. I tried to make sure God's angels were doing their job in every situation and that the devil and his demons were held back. I could pray for pastors and politicians the right way with the right Scriptures so that changes would have to take place. I would pray against this and for that and bind up this and loose that. Then I had all the right confessions ready at the end of each prayer. I was convinced that I was a lean, mean, praying machine.

In true prayer we don't go demanding; we go trusting.

Cliches, Formulas, and Magic Words

One day a few years later, while sitting in a service, the speaker went off topic for a moment. He said something that hit me so hard I didn't hear another word for the rest of the service. He said that prayer for many people had become a series of formulas and that their goal was, in reality, capturing darkness. He mentioned several prayer cliches and formulas and asked, "Why do we pray these things? Are they magic words that effect change?" Then he told the following story.

"You have guests staying the night at your home. In the middle of the night, you hear a huge uproar. Furniture is crashing, lamps are falling, and people are stomping about. You race out to see your guests running around with big green garbage bags in their hands, smashing into things. What would you say if, in explanation, they said it was too dark so they were trying to capture the darkness in the bags? You'd probably say, 'Why don't you just turn on the light!'"

That day I realized that I unwittingly believed that if you said all the right prayers in the right way, at the right time, you could somehow cause all the cosmic tumblers to fall into place and open the lock to answered prayer. My prayers weren't so much about getting to know God, talking to Him about my concerns, yielding my life to Him, or talking to Him about the hurts and pains of others, as they were about magic words spoken to achieve the desired outcome.

However, real prayer is about conversation with God, yielding ourselves to His will, and telling Him of our desires and concerns. In true prayer we don't go demanding; we go trusting. We don't barge into God's throne room with all the right words; we go in looking for God's love and mercy. We don't try to riddle the atmosphere around us with a nonstop stream of magic words, expecting somehow that God will bless our de-crees. We go in to a real, listening God, talking from our hearts and in our own words. We don't go in just to talk; we also go in to listen.

For months after I heard this speaker, when I got up in the morning to pray, I would sit quietly the whole time because I didn't know what or how to pray. Then I would just tell God how I felt or ask Him a question. Then once more I would be silent as I thought about God or the situation I had spoken to Him about. I started to come away from those prayer times with peace. After a while, I would come away with wisdom, my thoughts somehow being inspired and coming to a peaceful conclusion as I thought quietly in God's presence.

I had learned to say all the right prayers. Now I was learning to pray.

Simple Prayers from the Heart

This is a very important approach principle for teaching children. Children can easily learn formulas and phrases. We can teach them to pray long and hard with all the right words and tricks so they'll impress everyone's socks off. But we will be hindering them from learning to truly pray. They will be so caught up in their performance that relationship with God will be missed. We need to teach our children to speak from their hearts, to use their own words, to talk about things that concern or interest them. We can teach them to not always talk about things that require a yes or no from God or need any performance on His part. Also, we can teach them that sometimes it's okay to just sit and think while they're praying.

Keep it simple! Children's prayer lives or the words they use in prayer should not exceed their understanding of what they are saying; nor should they go beyond what they feel and know in their hearts. It's better to have our children pray two meaningful prayers and then go to sleep than to have them rattle off the tumbler-turning, lock-opening phrases that don't mean anything to them.

To draw a balance here, the Bible does tell us to pray about quite a few different things and to pray for them regularly. We need to teach our children to pray the different kinds of prayers the Bible calls us to. But our child's heart, trust, and love relationship with God needs to be encouraged so that it undergirds these other prayers.

As for me, I eventually got back to a balance in my own prayer life. I can pray for the things and people I should be praying for, but now my heart is turned to God. I'm listening, praying specifically for the things that are on my heart for people or situations and speaking as I would to a friend who could help. I'm praying in my own words, and each prayer is different from the one I prayed the last time. Prayer should be different each time: an exciting experience and an adventure with God.

If we push our children ahead of their hearts, we'll end up with good little prayer robots.

As we will discuss later in the book, when your children are young, they can benefit from learning "form" and memorized and/or formula prayers. Teaching children to pray Scripture and certain prayers or liturgy can add a real richness and diversity to their prayer lives. However, the loving relationship with a real God who is listening, who cares, and who desires to spend time with them is basic. These other prayers need to be built on and added to that relationship. If we push our children ahead of their hearts, we'll end up with good little prayer robots.

Children, as Jesus affirmed, are created and designed to be in relationship with God. We can't teach them "form," expecting relationship to come when they are older. Teach relationship first, and form will follow.

Reflections

1. What cliches, formulas, or magic words hinder your prayer life? Take a moment to make a list.

   _____

   _____

   _____

   What are some steps you can take to move beyond them?

   _____

   _____

   _____

2. What cliches, formulas, or magic words seem to hinder your children's prayer lives?

   _____

   _____

   _____

   How can you help your children move beyond them?

   _____

   _____

   _____

Get in Step with Your Kids

When my son, Joshua, was two, I sat down in the rocking chair with him. He was a fuzzy, cuddly little bundle with his one-piece pajamas covering everything from his toes to his neck. I got comfortable with Joshua snuggled up on my lap with his blanket. I was ready for prayer time. I began to pray about his future and his relationship with God, his friendships, and his growth as a person. All the while, Joshua, despite my gentle reminders, squirmed around like a cat caught under a wet towel.

I stopped and tried to explain that I was saying his prayers for him and he needed to be still and listen. When I said the words, "I'm saying your prayers," what seemed to be God's wisdom hit my heart. I was not saying his prayers—ones that he could understand, ones about things he might pray about—I was saying my prayers for him.

Joshua and I got settled again and I prayed this prayer: "Dear God, please help Joshua be a big boy and use his potty! In Jesus' name, amen." I chose something that Joshua was interested in, something current. I prayed simply and slowly and stopped before his attention span was spent. From that point on, Joshua was more interested in prayer than in squirming.

No matter what our children's ages, it is important to bring prayer down to their level. We need to keep it simple and build slowly. For Joshua, prayer was something his dad did—until I got in step with him and brought it down to a level he could understand.

Activity: Focus on Individual Concerns

What are some immediate, pressing issues for your children—such as learning to use the toilet or getting along with others at school—that you can use to draw them into prayer? Talk with each of your children on their own and come up with a list of concerns they have right now (not your concerns for them, but *theirs*).

_____

_____

_____

_____

_____

Then work through the list during your prayer times with them over the next week. Use this opportunity to teach your children that God cares about all of our needs, big and small.

Start with the Basics

When we first start praying with our children, some explanation of what we're doing and why is in order.

Keep the "what we pray about" very simple: We can pray about anything, anytime, anywhere, with anyone, in our own words.

An easy way to explain how and what to pray is to tell your children, "Talk to God just like you would talk to me. When you want something, you ask me for it. When you are upset, you come and talk to me so that I can fix things and make you feel better again. If you're upset with me, you tell me; if you need help, you ask me for it; if you don't understand something, you ask me to explain."

Prayer is as easy as that!

God loves our children even more than we do and He is their Father forever. Which leads to why we pray: God is love and He made us so that He could love us and take care of us. He wants us to talk to Him so that we can get to know Him better. He wants us to trust Him so that He can give us wisdom, teach us how He made things to work, take care of us, meet our needs, and lead and direct us in life. All so that we can have the best life possible.

> **We can pray about anything, anytime, anywhere, with anyone, in our own words.**

Put simply for young children, the reason to pray is this: God loves you and wants you to pray and trust Him so that He can show you His love and help you have a great life.

Questions

1. What are some ways you tend to complicate prayer, either for yourself or your children?

_____

_____

_____

_____

2. List five ways you can simplify prayer for yourself and your children.

_____

_____

_____

Ideas for Prayer
- Thank God for providing you with all the help you need for raising your children.
- Ask God to search your heart and show you any cliches, formulas, attitudes, thought patterns, and bad experiences that hinder you from drawing closer to Him. Commit these obstacles to God, and ask Him to break their power over your life.
- Ask God to open your eyes to see what things are hindering your children's prayer lives and how you can help them overcome these obstacles.

Prayer for Kids
Here is a sample prayer your children can use.

"Dear Father, please help me to be a good big boy/girl. Thank You for teaching me how to _____ and _____. Thank You for my mommy and daddy and all that they do for me. In Jesus' name, amen."

CHAPTER 5

Make It Fun and Normal

EXCUSE ME, ARE THEE AND THOU TWO OF GOD'S ANGELS?

Make It Fun and Normal

We sometimes are so . . . forced into cultural molds of how to pray that we forget that the basic thrust of prayer is celebration. It is a child coming to spend time with a Father who loves the child.

Steve Brown

Jesus prayed this prayer when He was raising His friend Lazarus from the dead: "Father, I thank you that you have heard me. I knew that you always hear me, but I said this for the benefit of the people standing here, that they may believe that you sent me" (John 11:41–42).

Simple prayer. Awesome results. Prayer is not about trying to sound holy or humble enough to get God to listen. One of the things Jesus disliked the most was hypocrisy. God doesn't want us to put on a show and all of a sudden be or sound like who we think He wants us to be.

God loves us and knows us better than we know ourselves. He wants us to come to Him in an honest, as-we-are, real way. Yes, He is God, and we need to come to Him with respect and give Him honor; but that respect should be the kind we expect from our children: behavior and words that are their own with an attitude that demonstrates their love, gratitude, and respect. God doesn't require that you change everything about yourself (words, tone, custom, or manner) like you would if you were addressing the Queen of England—no more than you would want your kids to bow or curtsey when entering your presence, call you "Oh Great Caregiver," and speak in a solemn voice with eyes on the ground. You would rather they find the balance of love, relationship, and respect.

You want your children to speak to you openly and honestly and be themselves; you also want them to speak respectfully and to remember who you are, who is in charge, and what you've done for them. That is what God wants from us.

When we teach our children to talk to God, we need to do it in a way that gets this idea across. If we always lower our voice an octave and talk like we once lived in Old England, they just think the whole exercise is weird. And we send them the message that God is distant and wants them to perform in His presence in order to earn His pleasure. If they think they must perform in front of a weird and different God, they may be hindered from building a love relationship with Him. On the other hand, we take our children beyond respect if we tell them, "If you're mad at God or you don't like the way things are going, just tell Him flat out. Yell at Him or get angry. God understands." We can be honest with God, but we should still be respectful.

Faith, a Sign of Respect

It's interesting to look at the different responses to God's messenger Gabriel that Mary and Zechariah, John the Baptist's father, had.

> Zechariah asked the angel, "How can I be sure of this? I am an old man and my wife is well along in years."
>
> The angel answered, "I am Gabriel. I stand in the presence of God, and I have been sent to speak to you and to tell you this good news. And now you will be silent and not able to speak until the day this happens, because you did not believe my words, which will come true at their proper time." (Luke 1:18–20)

"How will this be," Mary asked the angel, "since I am a virgin?"

The angel answered, "The Holy Spirit will come upon you, and the power of the Most High will overshadow you. So the holy one to be born will be called the Son of God." (Luke 1:34–35)

At first glance, it appears that both Mary and Zechariah spoke in their own words and asked the same simple question. But they didn't. Zechariah didn't so much ask a question as he said, "Hey, you'll have to prove that one to me. The odds are stacked against you with our age, you know!" He forgot for whom the angel was speaking. Mary, on the other hand, humbly received the message as truth and asked a simple question about the details. Mary received the answer to her question. Zechariah got struck dumb for about nine months.

Respect isn't a matter of words; it's a matter of the heart.

We know the questions Mary and Zechariah asked were different by how Gabriel responded. Respect isn't a matter of words; it's a matter of the heart. And, in this case, respect for God was measured by the confidence level these two had in God's ability and character—by their faith. Zechariah showed disrespect by the question he asked. Mary showed curiosity and confusion.

I would rather have my children think highly of me and my character, and therefore speak to me with love and respect, than have them say, "Yes, Dad" to everything I say but think and speak badly about me out of my presence. When we speak in reverent tones and words yet doubt God's love for us and His willingness and ability to help, we show our disrespect in a way similar to Zechariah's.

Let's teach our children to truly respect God and who He is—from their hearts, not merely from their lips. And let's teach our children to be themselves and speak to God in their own words. God wants our children to respect Him and understand who He is and what He can do so that they can trust Him more and He can demonstrate His love for them.

Reflections

How can you teach your children to respect God through your speech? Your actions? Your choices of entertainment? Write down a couple of ways for each of these.

_____

_____

_____

_____

_____

_____

Responsibility Can Be Fun

Once I came into my daughter Danica's room to say good night and found her reading her latest novel.

"Have you spent time with God yet?" I asked.

"No, Dad. I guess I should, but reading my Bible and praying is just not as fun as reading a novel."

Our children need to understand that spending time with and getting to know God should not be compared with entertainment nor measured by its excitement level. It's not always fun to go to school and learn, but if they don't, they will have limited career opportunities and life options. Sometimes we need to tell our sons and daughters: "I know eating properly isn't as much fun as eating ice cream and candy, but if you don't eat a balanced diet, you'll get sick and not be able to enjoy or live life properly. Your time with God is part of having a balanced life too."

In fact, that is exactly what I told my daughter. Then I added: "Some tasks really are for our own good. You may not want to get dressed in the morning—dressing is just too boring to be of consequence, but I guarantee that going to school in your pajamas will prove to be a little embarrassing."

With our children, we should be careful not to portray prayer as an option for those who choose to be holy or as some warm, nice, traditional thing to do at bedtime. Let's present prayer as a foundational and extremely important part of our children's lives. Of course, we should also present prayer as an awesome privilege and a great opportunity to get to know God and have Him care for us. But our children need to understand, without a doubt, that a strong prayer life is key to a growing relationship with God, which is key to a happy and fulfilling life here on earth and forever. We were created to know God, live with Him, receive His love, and grow and live under His care and direction. We cannot be fulfilled as people, enjoy life to the fullest, or really accomplish anything truly meaningful without that foundation. Prayer is not just an essential building block in our lives; it is the cornerstone. Building on any other foundation is building on sand.

Just because we need to eat broccoli doesn't mean we can't have a little cheese sauce on it.

When we remind our children of this and help them focus on it, they understand the reason and the necessity. We need to use simple language and images our children can understand to make clear that prayer is practical and basic to living. "Danica, prayer is the foundation. Building your life without prayer and relationship with God becomes as silly as spending your life eating nothing but candy. It's like never bathing, never learning, and never dressing."

Once our children understand this, it's time to make the teaching process fun. Just because we need to eat broccoli doesn't mean we can't have a little cheese sauce on it. It's a whole lot nicer to get dressed in the morning if we have some nice things to wear. It's also a whole lot more wonderful to go to school and learn if we have teachers who make the process fun and exciting. God did not mean for prayer to be drudgery. Yes, its purpose is more than enjoyment and greater than the purpose of entertainment in our lives, but learning prayer and praying itself can be fun and enjoyable. As we teach our children about prayer, we can make the learning fun as well as informative.

Here are some tips for making the teaching of prayer more enjoyable.

1. *Approach Prayer with Excitement*

Approach the topic of prayer and the prayer time with fun and excitement. When you say, "Let's pray," or "It's prayer time," make your voice upbeat and pleasant. Prayer is an exciting privilege, not a dreadful duty. Talking to God is real and awesome.

If your children start to resist or complain, stay upbeat; don't get serious and force it. Instead, reinforce the fun and excitement of God loving them and wanting to talk to them. Don't force them to pray; instead, say, "I'll say the prayer tonight." Pray quickly and simply, and move on to hugs or whatever comes next in the routine.

2. *Use Variety*

There may be a routine, but routine doesn't need to be boring. Any routine becomes that way only when mindless repetition sets in. Don't deal with boredom in routine by eliminating routine, because routine teaches discipline and provides a child with security. Instead, take the boredom out of the routine.

By purposely adding variety, you will avoid boredom, complaint, and stagnancy.

Plan to do things differently. Every once in a while, say your children's prayers for them. My wife and I do this if the kids have been up late on the weekend or are really tired. Instead of possibly forcing the issue with an overly tired child, we automatically avoid the potential complaints by saying their prayers for them. This also provides an awesome opportunity to teach by example.

Here are other suggestions. Every once in a while, instead of praying individually with your children, gather them together and have a family prayer time. Pray in a different place or in a different position. Go for a prayer walk together before getting ready for bed. Or, if your family likes to sing, sing a few hymns or praise songs to God as your prayer time. Have a "thank you" prayer time when you just take turns thanking God for different blessings in your lives. By purposely adding variety, you will avoid boredom, complaint, and stagnancy.

3. Remind Them of God's Love

Always let them know how much God loves them and desires to care for them. Make a regular habit of telling your kids at prayer time that God loves them and wants to hear from them, help them, and take care of them. Make it personal: "God loves you a lot."

It's equally important to reinforce God's love for your children as similar to your own love. Their knowing about God's unfailing love is the key that will unlock your children's desire to know God. Knowing about His love also will build their faith and trust—and help them *want* to talk to their loving Father.

4. Encourage Them in the Process

No matter what stage of learning your children are in, encourage them and praise them for their progress. After they finish praying, tell them how well they are doing. When they learn something new or take another step, let them know they did well. When they venture out and pray about things on their own, comment on it.

For instance, if they pray for a friend, tell them what a kind, compassionate thing that is to do and how God loves it when we pray for others. If they pray for wisdom, tell them how pleased God was when Solomon asked for wisdom, and tell them how pleased you and God are with them. Even if you need to correct them, reinforce the good they've done and then correct gently, letting them know that they are learning and doing well. When our teaching focuses more on encouragement and discovery than on correction and constant direction, it is ultimately more effective.

5. Make Prayer Time a Source of Comfort

Use prayer as a source of joy, blessing, and comfort. God is the good guy, not the all-seeing, guilt-inflicting, eye-in-the-sky who sees their every move. He should not be used as the police officer who takes over to force good behavior in the absence of parents. God doesn't want us or our kids to behave ourselves just because He's watching. Jesus said that to think a sin in your heart is to sin even though you didn't do it (see Matthew 5:27–28). God wants us to do things His way because we love and trust Him, knowing

He loves us and wants the best for us. We should never use God as our moral behavior baby-sitter.

Instead, we need to make sure we reinforce God as the good guy. Prayer is a key way to do that. When something good happens, without missing a beat we should thank God for His goodness. When our children are excited about something, we can take a moment to pray about it. This also reminds our children that prayer can take place anytime, anywhere. Not just at bedtime or not just at home.

> **We should never use God as our moral behavior baby-sitter.**

When we pray with our children about the exciting and good things that happen, we show them that God cares about what they care about. Similarly, if they are hurt or sad about something, we can take them in our arms and pray, asking God to help make them feel better and work things out for them. We should let Him be the comforter. (For young children, this should take priority over "kissing to make it better.")

6. Remind Them That Prayer Is a Great Privilege

We need to remind our children at every convenient opportunity how awesome prayer is, what a great privilege it is, and why we do it, reinforcing the reason and motivation for prayer.

God loves our children and wants them to get to know Him. He wants to teach them about life, direct them, and care for them. And as He desires to provide for us, so He desires to show our children His love so that they can have the best possible life, the way He meant it to be.

Prayer can be conversation and fun and reflect our children's personalities. At the same time, it can remain respectful. We can teach prayer as a necessary responsibility and also a privilege and a joy. As our children grow in prayer, they will start to sense God's presence, see His answers, and enjoy the relationship and the results. They'll become hooked on prayer, but we need to pave the way with love and creativity, demonstrating and presenting God in how we demonstrate and present prayer.

Questions

1. Make a list of the basic elements in your children's bedtime prayer routines, such as brushing teeth, putting on pajamas, and prayer. How can you alter or rearrange these elements to heighten your children's interest in prayer?

   _____

   _____

   _____

   _____

2. What are five things you can do for your children to show them that God loves them? Make a list and do one each weekday next week.

   _____

   _____

   _____

3. Close your eyes and think of God. What kind of picture comes to mind? Is he a kind old man? A stern judge? A loving Father? What characteristics come through the clearest?

   _____

   _____

   _____

   How do you think your perception of God affects your prayer life?

   _____

   _____

   _____

Activity: What's Your Picture of God?

Go through question 3 with your children. What are some of their images of God?

_____

_____

_____

Have each of them draw a picture of what they think God looks like. Discuss their drawings. How are they the same? How are they different?

_____

_____

_____

Use this exercise to discuss any negative or false views of God they may have.

Ideas for Prayer
- Thank God for the privilege of talking to Him through prayer.
- Ask God to help you see Him more clearly.
- Ask God to remove any negative images of Him that may be hindering your prayers or the prayers of your children.

Prayer for Kids

Here is a sample prayer your children can use.

"Dear Father, thank You for introducing Yourself to me. Please show me what You are really like. Help me to get to know You better. In Jesus' name, amen."

Making Progress

MOM, THE BABY IS PRAYING AGAIN.

CHAPTER 6

Making Progress

A man without prayer is like a tree without roots.

Pope Pius XII

One of the most important things to remember when teaching our children to pray is not to be in a hurry. There are at least four basic elements involved in the process of growing in prayer, and they all take time. Furthermore, all four need to progress together. If we force one ahead of the others, we can hinder the process. Only God can cause all of these areas to grow together, but by being aware of them we can help rather than hinder. Remember, relationship with God and growth are lifelong processes.

The four basic prayer elements our children will develop are:

1. *The "how-tos."* This element involves our child's actual prayers. It includes learning to pray all different types of prayer, learning to pray from the heart for the different things the Bible shows us to pray about, and learning to pray about everything.

2. *Their relationship with God.* This element involves learning to listen in prayer and learning to pray continuously. Here our children learn to desire fellowship with God, to love Him, and to want His will for their lives. It includes growing in their knowledge of God through Bible teaching, reading, and study.

3. *Their personal growth.* Personal growth means becoming more and more like God desires (and His Word teaches) them to be, growing in wisdom and character. Through prayer and fellowship they can display increasingly the fruit of the Spirit in their lives—the "love, joy, peace, patience, kindness, goodness, faithfulness, gentleness and self-control" that the apostle Paul listed in Galatians 5:22–23.

4. *Their growth in trust and faith.* Through this final element in the process, our children learn to trust God more and more. They learn not to hold anything back from Him. They increasingly talk to God and submit to Him in everything. They learn to see Him at work in their lives and gain an ever-increasing confidence in His love and actions on their behalf.

One Progressive Step at a Time

These four areas must develop together if our children are going to have healthy spiritual lives with corresponding benefits in all the other areas of their lives. If they learn the prayer how-tos before they develop other elements of prayer, their prayers will become a form or habit without a corresponding benefit. If they are encouraged to develop a spontaneous fun relationship with God, without encouragement in the other areas, they won't have the discipline and knowledge to keep the relationship growing. Personal growth without the other areas growing will tend to result in self-righteousness or a life with a self-help focus. And growth in trust and faith is simply impossible without the other areas growing. It's balanced growth that gets the results.

The most important prayer we can teach our children is to ask God to teach them to pray.

The process may sound complicated, but it isn't. God designed us to grow in all areas at once, and He is in charge of the process. Actually, the most important prayer we can teach our children is to ask God to teach them to pray. We can encourage them to address God and say something to the effect of, "I'd like to talk to you for a while. Can you help me pray?" Then have them wait a few seconds before starting. It may not make any difference to start with, but it will in the long run.

Rome wasn't built in a day. We need to take our children one progressive step after another. We need to stay consistent, stay sensitive to, and keep pace with our children's growth. Sometimes we think they need to know everything at once. But it's easier to build a solid wall by taking our time with each brick than to build it too quickly and have to spend even more time reinforcing it.

The rest of this chapter will cover some practical suggestions for accomplishing steady and solid growth in keeping with your child's response and character.

God Is in Control

We must teach our children that God is in control and wants them to grow in prayer and in relationship with Him. It's also important that we remind ourselves that He is in control of the teaching and learning process.

For years, in my desire to grow in my relationship with God, I struggled with spending time reading and studying the Bible and praying on a daily basis. For weeks or months I would be as disciplined as clockwork. Then my schedule would change or I would get distracted and time would go by without any daily devotions. When that happened, I would get mad at myself and ask God to forgive me. "I really wanted to do it, Lord, but . . ." And I would go over the list of excuses. Often my point seemed to be, "God, I want to do this, but I can't seem to make the time."

One day, while agonizing over this and making my excuses, I pictured in my mind what had happened: I had run down the stairs, ready to head out the door and, figuratively speaking, there would be God, sitting downstairs ready to meet with me. But when I saw Him, I'd say, "I'm really sorry. I can't make our appointment this morning. I'm really busy." And then I'd run out.

Two things struck me about the scene. First, I would never think of doing that to a friend, family member, or business associate. Second, I realized this was an issue of control. I asked myself, *Who is in control of the relationship?* If I was constantly calling you, coming over to see you, and trying to spend time with you, but you were always busy and kept putting me off, who would be controlling our relationship? You would be! Not only was I putting the Creator of the universe off, but I was presuming to be in control of the relationship.

So I prayed: "God, please forgive me for trying to control our relationship. You are in charge. You are my Father and Creator. I am Your son. Father, can You please make time for me and cause our relationship to grow and my time with You to be consistent? Father, I know that this is what You want, and I trust You to take over."

From that time on, my prayer and devotional life became both more consistent and better. Each day, I would pray and ask God if He would take time with me and set up our times together. If something happened and I missed my time with Him in the morning, I wouldn't condemn myself or ask God for forgiveness (implying again that I was in control). I would instead acknowledge that He was in control and ask Him to make time for us. Often God would provide the time. One day an appointment did not show, leaving me alone in my car between appointments with nothing to do—and there was my Bible on the backseat. Some nights I'd wake up unable to sleep and I would know it was time to be with God. And what an incredible time in prayer I would have, knowing that God had made the time and set up an appointment with me!

We need to look to God, asking Him to help us follow His lead for better times of fellowship and prayer. We also should allow Him to draw our children to Himself. This doesn't mean we drop the teaching ball—the process, diligence, and discipline. It does mean that we don't become worried and start to push when we shouldn't. We can rest in the fact that God loves our children even more than we do and is always working in their lives. If we'll do our divinely appointed part as parents and trust Him, He'll do His part.

We need to allow our children to grow slowly, at a pace that keeps up with their hearts, understanding, growth, and desire. If something we're doing feels like an uphill battle, we can stop, pray, and ask God for wisdom. Then we can slow down and find our way back to where our child's heart is, make it fun again, and start from there.

Reflections

1. Take a moment to examine your own relationship with God. Who is in charge? How can you tell?

   _____

   _____

   _____

   If it's you, how can you give control over to God?

   _____

   _____

   _____

2. What "uphill battles" are you facing with your children right now?

   _____

   _____

   _____

3. If you're not connecting with their hearts in your training, where do you think their hearts are?

   _____

   _____

   _____

4. How can you get back on track with them? Write down a couple of ways you can reverse the battle and make your training fun for your children again. Be creative. Have fun with it yourself.

_____

_____

_____

Prayer Is Individual

We love all our children, but every parent will agree that each of their children is unique and that they have a special but different relationship with each child. In every relationship we have as adults, not only is each one unique, but every relationship draws out of us different parts of who we are, so that we behave a little differently in each relationship. God does the same. He loves us all. Being love, He can't love some less, but He responds to and reveals Himself to each of our children differently, according to who they are and how they interact with Him. No two people God has created are exactly alike and no two relationships with Him can ever be the same.

That's exciting! As King David wrote, God formed each child in his mother's womb and by Him each person has been "fearfully and wonderfully made" (Psalm 139:13–14). What each has and can have with God can be equaled but never duplicated.

For our children, this means God made each to be born into this world absolutely original. With each child, He also created the potential for a unique relationship with Him like no other. The process for teaching a child to pray, which helps them enter into that special relationship, can therefore never be exactly the same as with any other child.

Here are some things you can do that will help you to match your teaching and training methods with each of your children's individual needs and traits.

1. *Talk to your children about God and prayer, and really listen to what they say.* Pick a relaxed time when you're alone with your

children and there are no distractions. Or better yet, if the children bring it up, you can take the time to hear them out.

Really listening and then responding to what they are saying about prayer and the process you're taking them through is the best way to make sure your approach is being tailored to each one. Listen closely to the meaning of their questions. Then answer their questions and pursue what is be-hind each one. And be careful to not become so caught up in the teaching process, achieving the goal or getting prayer time done, that you ignore their doubts and fears or push them past refusals to pray. Rather, talk it out with them, help them to understand, or together look up an answer to their question in the Bible. Most importantly, once you have talked with them, direct them back to God and have them respectfully share with Him their questions, fears, and doubts and ask Him for help. Ultimately, keeping the communication channels open between parent and child is key to keeping the communication channels open between God and child.

Each prayer training process should be unique and exciting.

2. *Listen to their prayer process preferences.* Some children will love to pray aloud. Some will want to pray softly and/or silently. Some will want to cut to the chase and go through their prayer list; some will want to yak on and on. Some will want to pray for others constantly; some will have trouble praying for others. It's important that we don't force our children into our mold or training process. Listen to their preferences and work your training around them. Encourage them in their strengths and gently help them move forward in their weak areas. Each prayer training process should be unique and exciting.

3. *Remember that God created different personality categories and gifting sets.* Understanding more about personality types can help us tailor our teaching and training to each of our uniquely made children by helping us understand how they think and operate. Good books on this topic can help us

grasp personality and gifting types in our children. (Two fine books are *The Way They Learn: How to Discover and Teach to Your Child's Strengths* by Cynthia Ulrich Tobias [Focus on the Family], and *The Treasure Tree* by John and Cindy Trent and Gary and Norma Smalley [Word].) But remember, our children should not be pigeonholed or pushed into the broad categories that personality-type studies give. Each child is an individual and these categories should be used only to understand key aspects of who each one is.

4. *Remember the rate of growth from one stage to the next will vary.* The growth in children's knowledge of the how-tos, relationship with God, personal growth, and growth in faith must dictate the process and the movement from one stage of learning to the next.

God designed our children for a unique and wonderfully special place with Him in His love and kingdom. Part of our teaching and training is helping them find that intimate relationship. In part 3 of this book, we will give suggestions for stages and for taking children from one stage to the next, but we must not let the stages dictate the growth rate.

Go for the Goal

For every learning and training process, there must be a goal. That goal is also the reward or benefit of the process. If our children are taking piano lessons, the goal is simply for them to learn to play the piano. To send children to a piano lesson without telling them about that goal would be confusing. Imagine if they had never heard the piano played and didn't know what it was for. Now someone instructs them to sit down, hold their hands a certain way, and strike the keys. It's all a meaningless process until the child knows that the piano is a musical instrument, hears it played beautifully, and is told that the object of their lessons and exercises is for them to learn how to play music like that. Now the child has a goal that promises the reward of good music. Similarly, we need to let our children know what the

We need to let our children know what the goal of prayer is.

goal (and benefit) of prayer is and what we are trying to accomplish with these lessons and exercises—a mature prayer life.

Jesus set the ultimate goal for us—and declared its benefit—in His prayer in the Upper Room: "Now this is eternal life: that they may know you, the only true God, and Jesus Christ, whom you have sent" (John 17:3).

Clearly, the main goal for prayer, and the biggest, most important goal in our children's lives, is for them to have a loving, vital, and intimate relationship with their Father God. Prayer is the communication channel that will help bring about that relationship. And that relationship results in many benefits.

Through our teaching and example we need to paint a vivid picture of what a mature relationship with God is and what it brings. Doing so lets our children know where all this prayer stuff is headed. When they understand and get excited about the goal, growth will be a natural part of achieving it.

Let's consider some pictures we can paint on the canvas of our children's hearts.

1. Your Best Friend

We begin by helping our children understand that God wants to become their best friend. Our children enjoy having friends, and God wants to come close to them, as a best friend would. You could explain this goal to your child this way: "God loves you a lot. He wants a special friendship with you that's different from anyone else. Wonderful friendships are built a little bit at a time, day by day. God wants you to come to Him every day and ask Him to help you get to know Him better.

"When we do this, we look forward to spending time with Him. Praying becomes one of our favorite things to do because we want to talk to Him about everything. As we spend more time with Him, He makes Himself more and more real to us, so prayer seems what it really is: time with our best friend and Father."

With this picture, we are telling our children that prayer isn't meant to be an impersonal, one-sided dialogue. There are two involved. When children ask, "Why can't we see God?" let them know that it was never God's will to hide from us, and that even though we can't see Him with our eyes, we can see with our hearts as we get to know Him better in prayer.

2. All That You Can Be

Like the slogan of the U. S. Army, God wants to help your child "be all that he or she can be." As you describe this goal for your children, remind them about their unique abilities. You might say, "God created you uniquely and gave you special talents and abilities. He has a plan for your life and wants to help you be the best 'you' that you can be. When we spend time asking God to give us His wisdom, teach us about life, and help us grow, He works inside us and in our lives to make that happen. And when we ask Him to direct our lives, we end up doing what He made us to do and living the best possible life we can have."

3. A Happy Life

A key goal every child would approve of is a happy life. And that is God's goal: true happiness founded in relationship with Him. You can describe this happy goal by beginning with a word most American teens have become comfortable with—awesome. Start this way: "God is awesome. He knows everything, and He sees everything and everyone at the same time. He knows the future and can do absolutely anything. And He wants to help you in every way that He can. He wants you to have a long and happy life,and He can give you the wisdom, help, guidance, and information that you need in every situation.

"Prayer, talking to and spending time with God every day, learning to ask Him about everything, and trusting Him, is the way God created people to get His help and have a happy life. No matter what happens, how we feel, or what we are thinking, God wants us to talk to Him about it, so that He can help and show us His love. The more we do this, the more God will help work out everything in our lives."

Remind your child that everything won't always be perfect. God said that we would have problems and troubles. But when we know how to pray, God will help us through and out of the problems and work everything out so our lives are good.

4. Great Relationships

Jesus said the two most important things in life are to love God and to love people. When we talk to God and ask Him to help us love people, and we start to pray for others, put others first, and let God help us be unselfish, an amazing thing happens: People start to love and appreciate us, and our lives get better. We—and our children—learn to truly love other people only when we get to know God and let Him teach and change us.

You could explain it to your children this way: "Do you want great relationships, so other kids appreciate you? When you get to know God better—when you feel His love—you start to learn to love, and that helps relationships. The result is that you end up having great friends and enjoying great friendships. And later, when you think about marriage, you will have some clues about what makes a good husband [or wife].

The goals for prayer sound a lot like the benefits of a relationship with God. They are!

"You will learn how to get along with and love everyone you meet, work with, go to church with, and live around; and you will end up being respected, loved, appreciated, and supported. This all starts to happen when we get to know God better in prayer, ask Him regularly to help us love, talk to Him about relationships, and ask Him to help others."

The goals for prayer sound a lot like the benefits of a relationship with God. They are! God's goals for prayer are for our benefit. Understanding these purposes and benefits will help our children know where prayer is taking them. And it will get them excited about getting there.

Questions

1. Think back to the four prayer elements discussed at the beginning of this chapter (page 81). How are your children progressing through these elements? Which areas require more emphasis?

_____

_____

_____

_____

2. Write the names of each of your children below (or at the top of a piece of paper). Under each name, list five characteristics that make that child unique.

_____

_____

_____

_____

_____

_____

What are some ways that you can use your children's uniqueness to heighten their interest in prayer? For example, if one of your children is very active and enjoys sports, how can you incorporate this interest into his or her prayer life?

_____

_____

_____

3. Write down the goal of prayer in your own words.

_____

_____

_____

How does this compare to some of the goals of prayer discussed in this chapter (pages 89–91)?

_____

_____

_____

Ask your children what they think the goal of prayer is. What are their answers? How are they the same as yours or this book's? How are they different?

_____

_____

_____

_____

_____

Ideas for Prayer

- Thank God for the uniqueness of each of your children.
- Ask God to help you to be a faithful teacher of your children.
- Ask Him to give you the wisdom, patience, knowledge, and encouragement you need to use their unique characteristics to draw them closer to Him.

Prayer for Kids

Here is a sample prayer your children can use.

"Dear Father, thank You for making me different from everyone else. Please help me to pray just like I'm talking to You from my heart. In Jesus' name, amen."

Mentor-Dad and Mentor-Mom

MOM IS SPENDING EXTRA TIME PRAYING, BUT IT WASN'T OUR FAULT.

Mentor-Dad and Mentor-Mom

The only time my prayers are never answered is on the golf course.
Billy Graham

When my oldest child was seven, she got up early one morning and found me praying. She sat on my knee and put her head on my chest. After greeting her cheerfully and giving her a hug, I told her she was welcome to stay, but I needed to finish my prayer time. I prayed out loud and she sat there quietly and listened. This happened every morning for about a week. And what a significant difference it made in her life! She became more interested in learning to pray.

Our children are always watching us. What we teach them with our actions will always have a more profound effect on them than what we merely teach with our words. The saying, "I'm sorry, I can't hear a word you're saying; the volume of your life is too loud" is especially true in parenting.

In addition to instruction—the how, what, when, where, why —our children need show-me-how and help-me-do-it training.

Such hands-on training occurs when they see "life in progress." This training by demonstration is especially important for practical and spiritual life skills: If we're telling someone this is an important part of life, then it had better be an important part of our own lives.

The current hot word for life training by example is mentoring or modeling. As parents, we *mentor* through our example and we *model God*. Be encouraged. We don't need to be perfect in order to raise spiritual children. In fact, effective mentoring requires that we depend wholly on God's grace and help in everything, especially parenting. Trying to pretend to be perfect will backfire on us because our kids know we're not. (We'll cover this more in chapter 9.)

There are three practical ways to mentor our children: (1) Mentor a life of prayer; (2) Mentor a right attitude toward prayer; and (3) Mentor reliance on prayer. Let's consider each of these.

Mentor a Life of Prayer

We must let our children see us pray. We may pray all the time, but if we always do it when the kids aren't around, or pray silently so they don't know we're praying, it might benefit us but it won't benefit their learning process. We need to come out of the closet for our children's sake—or at least let them know what we're doing in the closet.

Be Open

Show your children your prayer life. Try to coordinate your prayer time so that at least part of it happens when your children are awake and around. If you can't do this, when you're talking to them about prayer, let them know when you pray. Also, tell them individually that you prayed for them that day. This makes them feel loved and special, and you have communicated your life of prayer.

If your children are old enough to understand that you need to be left undisturbed for a time of prayer, and they can occupy themselves, they will see this is a priority as you disappear into your room for a while. However, don't leave them for a long time so they get bored and miss you. And don't choose a time that's usually spent with them. This could backfire and have them dislike prayer because it takes you away from them. It's best to try to coordinate a time to spend with them just before your prayer time, or just after, so they don't feel left out. This strategy will make it easier for them not to interrupt, because they know when you'll be spending time with them.

Today, with family schedules the way they are, it can be difficult to coordinate time for parents to pray. Each parent needs his or her own time; each can be a mentor in this area. The solution is to sit down as a couple and coordinate schedules. This way, one can take on the household and child responsibilities while the other is praying, and vice versa. We should never assume our spouses can get the time to pray during a working day or, if they stay home with the children, that they can fit prayer in.

> **Let the children know that you have an appointment with God.**

If you have no spouse to coordinate with, it's important to clearly set out the do-not-interrupt rules. Let the children know that you have an appointment with God and they are not to disturb you unless it is important. Be patient but firm. If they interrupt, hear them out patiently. Then go over the rules again and send them off without solving their nonemergency problem. Try not to get impatient and scold them while you're trying to pray. That will backfire too. It's like being caught behind the slow Sunday morning driver on your way to church. You finally pass the car and scream out your window, "What is wrong with you? Can't you see that I'm in a hurry to get to church!" Sounds funny, but being impatient with your children because they won't let you pray has the same negative effect.

Keep in mind too that if one of your children wants to sit quietly on your lap while you pray, it can be an excellent opportunity. Let that child know that he or she must sit still and be quiet and that if the child wants to leave, he or she can do so at any time (it's your prayer time). If more than one of your children want to do this, you can set up a turn system. (It's almost impossible to have your children concentrate when a brother or sister is inches away.) Older children may want to have their prayer time at the same time you do. If so, it's best not to make this a pray-together time, or you'll lose your needed time. Rather, let them be in the same room, quietly saying their own prayers.

Be Consistent

Whatever you do, you need to mentor consistency. If you're having trouble with consistency, these suggestions can help you get established in a regular prayer habit. Also, involving your children and letting them see your prayer life can be a real motivator. There's nothing like one of the children asking, "Why haven't you been having your prayer time lately?" to really keep you on the straight and narrow. But that's good. You should help and encourage each other toward spiritual things in your family.

If we do fall down in our regular habits, which we all do from time to time, we should ask for God's help and let Him take control of the relationship. Then, we can tell our children (they know anyway) that we got off track, but that we've prayed and are trusting God to help us keep our prayer schedule. (We may need to look at the time we put aside, too. The reason we stopped praying may be that the time we've scheduled is simply impractical.)

> **There's nothing like one of the children asking, "Why haven't you been having your prayer time lately?" to really keep you on the straight and narrow.**

Whatever we do, we mustn't make excuses! When we tell our children things like, "I've just been too busy to pray," or "Everyone keeps on wanting me to do something," or "I've been helping out at the church and/or helping other people," we are saying there are things more important than prayer and that prayer can be bumped. If we mentor that, our children will always find things that will bump prayer out of their lives. Prayer needs to be more important than eating, sleeping, and dressing. Such activities don't get pushed out because we all understand the benefits of keeping them in our schedules, and we understand the repercussions of leaving them out. Likewise, we need to establish the benefits of regular prayer and help our children understand the results of leaving it out.

Be Spontaneous

Another side of mentoring a life of prayer is showing children not only daily prayers but also all-through-the-day prayers.

One day, while driving with my children, something came up that I wanted to pray about. I proceeded to pray silently about the topic. As soon as I began, something I had never thought of before dawned on me (call me simple if you must): How were my children going to learn to pray all through the day and talk to God about their concerns and needs on the spot if they didn't hear and see Elaine and me doing it? Instead of praying quietly, I casually told the children what I was thinking and said I thought we should pray about it. Then I prayed very briefly about the situation and went right back to what we were doing and talking about.

The children enjoyed being included and being asked to help with something that Dad thought was important. From that day on we have made a habit of mentoring spontaneous prayer. It may seem awkward at first, but it demonstrates to our children that prayer is real, important, and foundational to everything in our lives. Praying only at one time in the day can make prayer seem like an afterthought, necessary to get God to sprinkle His blessings on what we've done. Mentoring all-through-the-day or spontaneous prayers will help us to better demonstrate what prayer is really about.

This is important because children, for the most part, live in the moment. Getting to the end of the day and trying to get them to remember the needs of others they witnessed or concerns they had during that day, can be difficult. Children need to learn to pray on the spot, when the reason for prayer is now.

Mentor a Right Attitude Toward Prayer

It's relatively easy to teach something to our children when we make a continuous effort to do so. However, mentoring goes further. True, it includes what we intentionally teach and model. But it also includes what we are teaching and modeling every other moment of the day. What we teach our kids when we aren't actually setting out to teach them anything is harder to keep tabs on and control. But it is crucial.

Our attitudes, automatic behavior, and responses are huge indicators of what we really believe. Our children seem to have a built-in tracking system that reads these automatics and traces them right back to what is really in our hearts.

If prayer is still a labor and struggle rather than a joy for us, we can ask God to help us learn to love and enjoy prayer. Prayer is not meant to be an annoying but necessary infringement on our lives. Prayer is meant to be the greatest blessing, opportunity, and pleasure in our lives.

Once we are changing and have a growing love of prayer, we need to pass it on to our children. Here are some tips that might help.

1. *Spend time with God.* When you spend time with God on a regular basis, it will make a difference in who you are, the way you feel, and how you behave. The psalmist tells us that we will be filled with the joy of his presence (Psalm 16:11; 21:6). And through our prayers and petitions, "the peace of God, which transcends all understanding, will guard your hearts and your minds in Christ Jesus" (Philippians 4:6–7). You will notice the difference in your life and so will your kids! You can use the changes you see in yourself to encourage your children about the benefits of prayer.

2. *Share your insights.* When you come from prayer, it's great to share with your children what you learned or experienced during that time with God. You can talk about something you thought for the first time while praying, about what you're trusting God for that excites you because you know He's taking care of it, or about the peace you felt while praying.

3. *Choose a good time.* It's crucial to choose a good time to talk to your children about these things. Announcing that you had such a good time praying today that you're canceling the special dinner you had planned so you can tell them all about it will backfire. That seems obvious, but sometimes you may violate this approach principle because you don't recognize the things that are really important to your kids. If you remember the principle, you'll know by the look on their faces or their reaction whether you've chosen a bad time. It's much better to back off and wait for a better time.

A good time for new and exciting prayer information is just before saying prayers with your children at night when this is an expected topic. Speaking of bedtime prayers, be careful not to drag your tired, worn-out, woe-is-me self into your child's bedroom, then grump and speed your way through their prayer time so you can get on with relaxing. If you feel that way, it might be a good idea to ask your spouse to take over. (But don't let your children hear you bartering over who has to do the prayer thing tonight. That could be misunderstood.) Or you can ask God for strength, remind yourself of the importance of the process, and use all your leftover energy to get excited about your child's prayer time.

4. *Seize the moment.* When your children ask you to pray about something with them or for them, praise them and get excited about talking to God about the issue. You may be busy or really beat, but when your children are asking for prayer, not only is what you're doing working, but this is the best time to pray and teach. They're primed to learn!

5. *Throw an "Answer Party."* When God answers a family member's prayers or a family prayer, big or small, have a little impromptu party. Thank God and then get excited, talk about it, and do something to celebrate: have a favorite dinner, plan a special outing, or let the kids have some friends over to join in the fun. Any task that you learn to do, and then do, needs a payoff. Having your prayers answered is a big payoff for prayer, and celebrating the payoffs make them more memorable and exciting for your children. The reward of the payoffs should outweigh the disciplines of learning the task.

Reflections

1. What kinds of prayer attitudes and behaviors are you modeling to your children through your own prayer life?

_____

_____

If you're really brave, try asking your children. What do they say? Did they answer the way you were expecting?

_____

_____

_____

2. What are some ways that you can improve the example you
    are setting? For example, do your children ever get to see you
    pray, or do you always do it behind closed doors?

    _____

    _____

    _____

3. Together with your children, come up with a "top ten" list of
    bad excuses for not praying. Have fun with it. Then make a
    list of ten reasons why you should pray.

    _____

    _____

    _____

Mentor Reliance on Prayer

We need to let our children into our prayer lives! We can do this
many ways: by telling stories, doing family prayer projects, and
letting them watch us respond to difficult times.

Faith Stories

My children, like all children, love stories. Once I told my children
a true story about a time I asked God for twenty dollars and how He
miraculously provided it for me. The children just loved it and asked
me to tell them more stories like it. We ended up calling true stories
of answered prayer "Faith Stories." Faith Stories became a great vehi-
cle to teach prayer and get my children excited about it. Now the
most requested type of stories in our family are Faith Stories.

A very important part of the mentoring process is sharing our
past: how we got from there to here and what we learned in the

process. Faith Stories are a great way of mentoring our children from our past experience. They give the opportunity to take the lid off our prayer lives and let our children learn from what we've learned.

What was the first thing we ever prayed for? What was the first (and/or most spectacular) answer to one of our prayers? How did we learn to pray? Did we struggle with praying regularly? Have we ever sensed God's presence in a very real way? Have we received God's wisdom for a specific situation in answer to prayer? Have we prayed for others and seen results? What led us to realize that prayer and our relationship with God were foundational to our lives? All those are legitimate questions that, honestly answered, let our children see into God's working in their parents' lives.

Let our children see into God's working in their parents' lives.

My friend and editor told me a story that helped to inspire her faith. "One day when I was quite young, my missionary father was asked to fetch the police to help put down a tribal conflict around our mission station. On his way down the lane in a borrowed Volkswagen, a warrior threw a spear at him. It lodged in the rubber between the window and the doorframe. When he was clear of the conflict, my father stopped and removed the spear. We found out later that, given the time changes, at the exact time my father was driving down the lane between the warring factions, in General Motors in Canada my grandfather felt a strong urge to pray for Dad. He dropped to his knees and prayed. And God kept my father safe. We certainly learned God answers prayers!"

It's a good idea to write out a list of Faith Stories; jot down one or two sentences for each one, just enough to remind you of the story. Then begin using your story collection with your children.

A wonderful thing can happen after you've told a few Faith Stories. Your children may want to experience, and then tell, their own! They will get excited when they have one to tell.

Faith Stories in Progress
The next step to letting our children into our prayer lives is telling "Faith Stories in Progress." One night, when I was quite

tired (yet mustering up the energy to be excited about prayer time), one of my daughters insisted that I tell her a Faith Story. Without thinking, I told her I didn't have a new one because I was right in the middle of a Faith Story.

As soon as I said it, the challenge hit my heart: "Why not tell her what is going on and what I am trusting God to help with?" Of course, the "what if" fears came screaming immediately into my head. But I argued back the what-ifs with a few so-whats—God doesn't need me to protect His integrity. If I could trust Him in the situation, then I could let my daughter be part of it. Even if that meant that at the end of the story I needed to teach her that sometimes God doesn't always work things out the way we want Him to.

Sure enough, before my mental gymnastics were even over, my daughter asked me to tell her my "Faith Story in Progress." It was a financial story, and before the week was out God had wonderfully taken care of the situation. He did it in a way that had His fingerprints all over it. My daughter, after sharing in the problem, was even more excited about the answer.

It is crucial to let our children know what we're praying about. And it's important to give them specifics and ask them to pray for us. The next step is to keep them abreast of our progress and tell them the story once it's no longer an in-progress one.

Reflections

Every Christian has at least one faith story to tell—an incident where God answered your prayers or intervened in your life in some sort of extraordinary way. What are some of your faith stories? Sit down with a notebook and ask God to bring some of your faith stories to mind. Jot down the following details about each story:

Date: _____

Circumstances:_____

_____

_____

My thoughts and prayers:_____

_____

_____

Verses that helped me:_____

_____

_____

God's answers: _____

_____

_____

Lesson(s) learned: _____

_____

_____

Application for my children: _____

_____

_____

Once you begin compiling your list of faith stories, look for opportune moments to share them with your children. For example, if your children are struggling with worry, share a story about a time when you were tempted to worry but chose to put your faith in God instead. Tell them how this helped you deal with the situation and how God showed Himself to be faithful.

Family Prayer Projects

"Family Prayer Projects" is another way to let our children into our prayer lives and mentor them thereby. When something comes up that concerns the whole family, like moving, having to find a new house, needing another car, or finding a church home, we can gather everyone together, talk about the situation, and write down what we want to ask God. Then we can pray together, ask for wisdom, and ask God to direct and/or provide. As a family we can be still in God's presence and thank Him for hearing and answering our prayer.

Keep it simple and brief. Then don't forget to keep everybody up-to-date on what happens. And when God finishes working out everything, be sure to have a thank-you prayer time and an Answer Party together.

Activity: Family Prayer and Answer Book (or Board)

What are some events or circumstances in your life that could become family prayer projects? Make a list of potential prayer projects and discuss them with your children.

_____

_____

_____

You may even want to create a family prayer record book, prayer calendar, or white board to keep a visual track of what you pray and how God answers. Find a system that works for you. It could be with Post-It® Notes that stay up until answered, a white board, or anything else that works. Hold a "thanksgiving party" every time a prayer is answered. Pray together and renew your previous prayers with your family at a regular time each week. Watch your family's excitement grow as God answers your prayers one-by-one.

Fielding Curve Balls

The most crucial time to mentor our reliance on prayer is probably when life throws us a curveball, big or small. When life seems to be giving us a blow to the head and/or God seems not to be answering our prayers, our children watch very closely. They need to see us in prayer, not despair. Our faith will be tested; so will theirs. It seems a contradiction, but the most important time to mentor reliance on God is when God doesn't seem to be very reliable. During those confusing and difficult times, your response of faith becomes a powerful mentoring tool.

The words of James and Peter can sustain us during those difficult times:

Consider it pure joy, my brothers, whenever you face trials of many kinds, because you know that the testing of your faith develops perseverance. Perseverance must finish its work so that you may be mature and complete, not lacking anything. (James 1:2–4)

In this you greatly rejoice, though now for a little while you may have had to suffer grief in all kinds of trials. These have come so that your faith—of greater worth than gold, which perishes even though refined by fire—may be proved genuine and may result in praise, glory and honor when Jesus Christ is revealed. (1 Peter 1:6–7)

Once, many years ago, when Elaine and I were starting our publishing business, a financial emergency came up. We did all we knew to do, and we took the matter to God. After some time praying and waiting, we both thought God was going to meet our need. The need was large and it had a time limit. On the final day—we needed the money by 8:00 A.M. the next morning—I did everything I could think of. Throughout the day, whenever I would start to feel it was hopeless, I would turn to God in prayer and quiet myself again, choosing to trust even though the looming consequences of missing the deadline were not very pleasant. I had figured that the money had to come by mail or courier. So I set 5:00 P.M., the end of the working day, as the time it needed to be there.

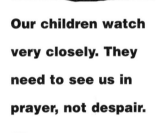

Our children watch very closely. They need to see us in prayer, not despair.

At 4:50 P.M., I left prayer and went into despair. I was praying, if you could call it that, but my prayers were whines and complaints and were filled with such faith-filled statements as "Why me?" "Woe is me!" and "Where are you?" Ten minutes after my fit in God's presence had started—at exactly 5:00 P.M.—the phone rang. I pulled myself together and answered. A courier, who had never delivered to my post office box, had just shown up there with an envelope for me. The check inside was more than enough to take care of the financial emergency and our other needs as well.

I felt "lower than the belly of a pregnant ant." God forgave me because He loves me. He turned my embarrassment into a blessing. Ever since then, whenever I'm in the middle of a Faith Story, I have the strength not to despair because I know that God is faithful and His answer could be only ten minutes away.

The old saying, "When life hands you lemons, make lemonade," can be applied here. If we have the opportunity to trust God against all odds, let's not run away. Our children are watching, and during such times we can honor God by running toward Him. By mentoring a correct response to tests and trials, we are equipping our children to face anything life can throw at them. It's an awesome opportunity!

Questions

What are some potential curve balls that life can throw at your children? What prayer habits can you help your children develop now to help them handle these obstacles more effectively?

_____

_____

_____

Ideas for Prayer
- Think back on some key answers to prayer that you have received over the past few months and thank God for His faithfulness.
- Ask God to help you to model a positive attitude toward prayer.
- Ask God to remind you to consult with Him before making decisions.
- Ask God to teach you how you can lead your children into a deeper relationship with Him.

Prayer for Kids

Here is a sample prayer your children can use.

"Dear Father, please help me to remember to talk to You first whenever I have a problem or when I need help. In Jesus' name, amen."

Modeling God

WELL, DAD SAID NO AND YOU SAID NO; NOW I'M GOING
TO GO ASK GOD.

CHAPTER 8

Modeling God

Is prayer your steering wheel or your spare tire?

Corrie ten Boom

Teaching our children to pray by being parental mentors, especially mentoring by example, can be powerful. There is another effective form of mentoring: modeling God. This is a mirror that helps our children understand God and prayer better. Let me explain.

Our children can't see God, but they can see us. We teach them God is their heavenly Father, that He is like another parent.

At first, our children are going to see God as they see us. God is the One who called Himself our heavenly Father and thereby created a model of Himself in us. In other words, we have a responsibility to act like God would act toward and in front of our children in order to give them the proper picture of who God is. We can become a mirror, reflecting God who is in us.

God wants our children to be like Him and His Son, Jesus. But God doesn't only want them to learn by His and Jesus' example;

He wants them to learn to be like Him from our example.

This type of modeling has two very significant areas of application in teaching our children to pray. We can model godly service, and we can model showing God's love.

Models of Godlike Service

God As Servant

When Jesus and His disciples gathered together for the Passover, Jesus surprised and even shocked them. He got up from the table, took off His outer garments, put a towel around His waist, and washed their feet. Walking on hot dusty roads all day in sandals made feet very dirty. The job of washing them usually was reserved for the lowliest of the servants. In the absence of servants, you would think some of the disciples might have thought to do the task or at least offer to wash their Master's feet. But the disciples still did not understand Jesus' words: "The greatest among you will be your servant. For whoever exalts himself will be humbled, and whoever humbles himself will be exalted" (Matthew 23:11–12).

They argued over who would be the greatest in Jesus' kingdom. To wash even their Master's feet would have been to take the lowest position in the room. So, to make His point again and to demonstrate God's love and attitude, Jesus took that position. After He was finished, He asked His disciples if they understood what He had just done. "I'm your Teacher and your Lord and I washed your feet. You also should wash one another's feet" (see John 13:13–14).

With that one action, Jesus demonstrated what someone in a position of authority is to be like. He put our needs, desires, and welfare ahead of His own. He spent His earthly life serving God and others; then He suffered the most brutal of deaths so that we could live.

I'm sure His disciples thought they were to serve Him: surely the greatest is served! They must have thought Jesus taught and healed so that He could become great, well-known, and powerful—so He could set up a kingdom, as man understands it, for Himself on earth. But in reality, His every action—every hour in prayer, every teaching, every act of love, every miracle—all were done to serve His disciples and those who would become His disciples. Not a single thing Jesus did was for Himself. With the heart of a true leader and a truly great person, He served others completely.

He brought this to the disciples' attention by washing their feet. Then He told them to do likewise.

God is love. Everything He has done in creating earth, His continual working and patience to bring us back to Himself, and the sending of His own Son, have all been for our sake, not His. When God says, "And I will be your God," He means, "I will love you and care for you; I will bless you and serve you."

> **When God made us parents, He made us servants of the next generation.**

Parents As Servants

"No servant is greater than his master" (John 13:16). As God's followers, we should also serve. When God made us parents, He made us servants of the next generation. When God gives authority, He gives the same responsibility that He takes on Himself: the responsibility to unselfishly give, love, care for, and serve those we have authority over. The more you are a servant, the more you lay aside your needs and desires to put the needs of those you have authority over ahead of yours.

We have a duty to model God's loving, caring, serving attitude to our children. If we bring them up with the worldview the disciples had—those who are great and are in authority don't serve but are served—how will they come to understand and through prayer receive God's love and service to them? By our actions, we must show that the first (or those who put themselves first) shall be last, and the last (or those who put themselves last and serve others) shall be first.

My point is made clearer by all of you who are reading this and feeling uneasy whenever I say God wants to "serve" us. We've been brought up in a world that says a servant is lowly and a great person is served. But Jesus reversed it and said by word and example, "The greatest serves. The greatest thing you can do is serve, care for, and love others." Service is the key to relationship, love, and life. It is who God is, how He thinks, and how He made everything to work. To really live is to learn to serve.

God wants us to model Him as a loving, giving, and serving Father who asks nothing for His own good or out of selfishness but only what benefits us. His every thought and motivation is for our good.

When we ask our children to do something, it should be because we are training them and helping them, never because we are too lazy to do it ourselves. When we teach them, we should do so to give them the best possible life, not so they can finally get smart and make our lives easier. When our children request something, our answer should be only to benefit their needs and best interests, not what serves us best or is convenient. To model a loving heavenly Father who answers prayer, we must answer our children based on one question: What is best for them? If as servant parents we lay down our lives for our children, we will be amazed by the results.

Service is the key to relationship, love, and life. To really live is to learn to serve.

Sometimes our children will try to talk us out of an answer we've given them. The reason? They know what is fair and reasonable. Indeed, 99 percent of the time that we reverse the answer, it should have been different to start with, but we said no without thinking about them or considering ourselves their servants.

By the way, if you're wondering when I was going to write the balancing comments, here they come. When you lay down your life for your children, you can now, like Jesus, teach them to do the same for you and others: "Submit to one another out of reverence for Christ" (Ephesians 5:21).

Reflections

1. Think about some of the reasons service might be hard for you. For example, do you feel diminished by it, as if service means your personal value is less than the one served? Or perhaps you feel it will undermine your authority with your

children? Write down a couple of the attitudes, assumptions, or beliefs that make serving your children difficult.

---

2. Now make a list of things you can do to address these things and bring yourself closer to Jesus' attitude. How can you act through your assumptions or attitudes? What can you do to change them?

Models of God's Love

The "Love Chapter" of the Bible, 1 Corinthians 13, contains beautiful sentiments. Verses 4–8 have been written on plaques and posters and been the object of many calligraphers' pens and countless readings at weddings, anniversary parties, and other special occasions. They have been used so much, it seems, that they have almost become beautiful poetry to be admired as opposed to practical advice to be followed. But the five verses are simply descriptions of how we should model God's love. Here they are, with key aspects separated for emphasis:

> Love is patient, love is kind.
> It does not envy, it does not boast.
> It is not proud. It is not rude.
> It is not self-seeking, it is not easily angered.
> It keeps no record of wrongs. Love does not delight in evil
>   but rejoices with the truth.
> It always protects, always trusts, always hopes, always
>   perseveres.
> *Love never fails.* [Italics added]

One day, while reading these verses and thinking over practical applications, I noticed something that has helped me get a handle on them. (I don't know how well the original Greek, sound hermeneutics, and traditional theology support my practical application, so take the following as inspiration rather than doctrine.) I'm sure that all of the elements, attitudes, and actions of love written in these verses interrelate, but I noticed that the five pairs describing real love seemed to relate in a very practical way.

Love Is Patient and Kind

Look at the first pair. Patience is inward and kindness is outward. It seems that when we become impatient we tend to be unkind. I've noticed that when my words, and therefore my tone toward my children, become unkind, it's usually because I've become impatient with them or the surrounding circumstances.

One night I wasn't doing a very good job of mustering up the energy for prayer time, and I got impatient with the learning process. I spoke unkindly to my child and got up to leave. As I was leaving, I realized that in the process of trying to teach my children how much their heavenly Father loves them I, their earthly father, was acting unkindly toward them. What a contradiction! I spun on my heel, went back, got down on my knees beside my child's bed, and asked her to forgive me. Then I spent extra time and poured out extra love, patience, and kindness toward her in order to model God to her.

Love Doesn't Envy or Boast

Envy comes out of insecurity and selfishness. When we envy, the flip side is that we boast to try to prove we have better and are better. We must be careful as parents not to put our children down because of our insecurities and compare them to ourselves or others. "You think you have it bad! When I was a kid, we had to walk uphill both ways for ten miles in four feet of snow with cardboard boxes for shoes in order to get to school!" These kinds of comments don't come alongside and build. They pull down.

Love Isn't Proud or Rude

Pride causes us to think we are better than others. When we think we are superior, we end up being rude. When we are rude, we need to check for pride. We can be rude with our children and say things that cut and hurt when we see them as slow or immature compared to ourselves. "Can't you understand this?" "How many times do I have to tell you?" "What are you, stupid or something?"

We should humble ourselves with our children and lovingly build them up, knowing that we're also still learning. We need to model a God who loves us and encourages us even though we don't know a fraction of what He does.

Love Is Not Self-Seeking or Easily Angered

During a sermon by one of my pastors, he said that anger is rooted in selfishness. We get angry because things aren't going our way, the way we wanted, or as fast as we wanted. When something or someone opposes our agenda, we feel angry. As soon as we see signs of anger welling up inside, we should ask ourselves how we can stop focusing on ourselves and instead think of the needs, desires, and agendas of others.

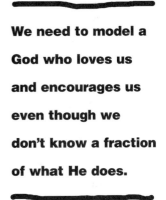

We need to model a God who loves us and encourages us even though we don't know a fraction of what He does.

There are times, even after being lovingly taught and instructed, that our children will continue to do something that will hurt them. At such times we need to be angry. But this anger is not selfish. It is slow to ignite and has to do with our love for our children not focusing on ourselves. However, the majority of the time we express anger to our children we can trace it back to us being self-centered. At such times we need to stop and refocus on the objects of our care and love, our children.

Love Keeps No Record of Wrongs and Rejoices in Truth

Every time we keep track of a wrong, remember it, and bring it up again to make a point, we are delighting in evil. That mistake has become our tool: a wonderful little tidbit to use to manipulate and control its owner.

Instead, love rejoices with the truth. It encourages. It instructs the ones who make the mistakes and helps them move beyond, never looking back. It also means that love focuses on the right things people do and encourages them forward instead of banging them on the head with their wrongs. As our children's mentors, we should model a God who always forgives, who encourages us forward no matter how badly we fail.

Love Always . . .

The next four statements in these verses seem to work together with the conclusive ending of the section to sum up all that has been said.

"It always protects, always trusts, always hopes, always perseveres." The Bible says that God is love. He will always protect (defend and support us). He will always trust (think the best of us and trust us to do the right thing). He will always hope. That means He will hang on to a good outcome for us; He never gives up on us. Finally, God always perseveres. He keeps working, loving, and caring for us no matter what.

As parents, we need to become models of God to our children by always protecting, defending, and supporting them. We will think the best of them and trust them to do the right thing. We will always hope, hanging onto a good outcome for them, and never giving up on them. In our love, we will always persevere, continuing to try, train, teach, care for, and direct them, no matter what.

When we model God and His love, we cannot fail to bring the best results.

Finally, love always triumphs. "Love never fails," the Scripture declares. I've seen families who focused on all the rigors of spiritual discipline but were short on love. I've seen families short on spiritual discipline and long on love. The families I've seen with the love focus come out ahead. But the most impressive family results I've ever seen are in a family that practices love, lovingly teaches spiritual discipline, and grows in God's grace and love together. Faith works by love, according to the Bible. In contrast, the apostle John said, "If anyone says, 'I love God,' yet hates his brother, he is a liar" (1 John 4:20).

We need to model a God who loves unconditionally, cares for

constantly, and teaches, trains, and disciplines without wavering, and who always does it for our good.

God is love. Love never fails. When we model God and His love, we cannot fail to bring the best results.

Question

What are five ways you can serve your children? Make a list and do one each weekday next week.

_____

_____

_____

Activity: Love, Service, and Prayer Calendar

For a long-term commitment, you may want to create a love and service calendar for your children and give it to them this year. Here's how you make it: Buy a calendar that you know your children will enjoy looking at. Go through the calendar and mark down special family events, such as birthdays, holidays, anniversaries, and so on. Mark a couple other days in each month "just because." For each of these special days, come up with a way that you can show your love to your children and/or serve them in some way. It may be as simple as giving them a coupon for a hug on that day, or it may be arranging some sort of special activity, event, or secret surprise that they can look forward to doing with you. It could simply be some one-on-one time with you. Give the calendar to your children as a gift (possibly for Christmas) and have them hang it in a central place in the home so they can keep track of what they have to look forward to each month.

Ideas for Prayer

* Thank God for demonstrating true love through the life of Jesus.
* Ask God to show you how to love and serve your children.
* Ask Him to help you to demonstrate your love to them in everything you say and do.

Prayer for Kids

Here is a sample prayer your children can use.

"Dear Father, thank You for my parents. Please help Mom and Dad teach me about You and show me what You're like. In Jesus' name, amen."

Amazing Grace

DOES GOD SLEEP IN ON SATURDAYS? I HAVE SOMETHING
I WANT TO PRAY ABOUT.

Amazing Grace

Dear Lord, help me get up; I can fall down by myself.

Jewish Proverb

In the beginning of part 2, I told you that help was on its way if you were starting to feel like this book was demanding too much of you. Now having read most of this section, you may be thinking: "He's telling me, 'Be perfect, be a good example, love your kids, mentor a great prayer life—and have it all done by next Monday. And could you solve a few of the world's political problems in your spare time between now and then?'" Of course, none of us is going to be perfect by next Monday; that is not what spiritual parenting is about.

I want to describe a resource I rely on absolutely. In fact, without it I would be lost as a parent. It's *grace parenting*, or parenting by God's grace.

God's Job

To understand *grace parenting*, or the power of God's grace in rearing godly children, let me recount one aspect of my early

Christian experience. When I first became a Christian, I was a prayer meeting waiting to happen. One kind person has described me with the words "spiritual space cadet." I wanted so much to please God, to do everything right and be perfect overnight, that the slightest mistake on my part would send me into a self-condemning tailspin. I got to the place where I felt like I just couldn't do it anymore. I was ready to give up. Then someone gave me a book by Andrew Murray. After I had finished round fifteen of Rick versus Rick, I picked it up to read.

When we yield ourselves to God, He lovingly works change in our hearts and souls.

While I was reading, I came across Philippians 2:13: "For it is God who works in you to will and to act according to his good purpose." That verse jumped off the page and everything inside me seemed to yell, "It's not *Rick* at work causing Rick to want to do God's will and then causing him to do it. It's *God* doing it! It's His job."

The dam broke and I cried for a long time, realizing that all that self-reliance was killing me. Jesus died, not just to solve the sin problem but to put us back in relationship with a Father who loves us and will work with us and in us, lovingly causing us to grow and become all that He created us to be. We don't give up; we give in. We let God's love and Jesus' work on the cross be what carry us forward, not our own righteousness and effort. When we yield ourselves to God and put our lives and growth in His hands, by His Holy Spirit He lovingly works change in our hearts and souls.

After that, I looked in my Bible for more about God working in me and through me. Here's just a bit of what I found:

[May God] equip you with everything good for doing his will, and may he work in us what is pleasing to him, through Jesus Christ, to whom be glory for ever and ever. Amen. (Hebrews 13:21)

May God himself, the God of peace, sanctify you through and through. May your whole spirit, soul and body be kept blameless at the coming of our Lord Jesus Christ. The one who calls you is faithful *and he will do it.* (1 Thessalonians 5:23–24, italics added)

I will give you a new heart and put a new spirit in you; I will remove from you your heart of stone and give you a heart of flesh. And I will put my Spirit in you and move you to follow my decrees and be careful to keep my laws. (Ezekiel 36:26–27; see also 1 Corinthians 15:10 and Philippians 1:6)

God has committed to work in us and effect the change necessary for us to live His way and receive His blessing. All we need to do is trust Him and yield to Him as we move forward. We need to ask Him to work in us in any and every area we need help in. That includes parenting. He gives us grace to rear our children, grace that includes wisdom and becoming all that we can be as parents.

Reflections

1. Take a few minutes to think about these verses (you might also want to look up the others mentioned). What are some areas where this truth of God's work in you can set you free or release you from anxiety?

   _____

   _____

   _____

2. What are some moments or situations as a parent when you feel you really need God's grace? How can you make yourself more open to receiving God's grace at those moments?

   _____

   _____

3. How can you come to trust God more? Are there some ways you can yield more to Him as you move forward?

   _____

   _____

Grace Parenting

Our children are fearfully and wonderfully made, each one a unique design of almighty God. They are the crown of His creation, so wonderfully complex that scientists, psychologists, and those in medicine haven't begun to unravel the mysteries of their design and workings. Knowing that, we need not fear that God wants us to raise our children without His help and wisdom. How can we imagine that we would even know how?

God at Work in Us

God wants us to ask Him to work in us to make us the best parents we can be. He desires to give us the wisdom, understanding, and day by day help that we need to complete this awesome task. We won't be perfect, but when God is working in and through us and we're relying on His grace, He has a way to cover our mistakes and wonderfully work everything out.

Introducing our children to God and teaching them to pray is the most awesome responsibility inside of the most privileged task of parenting. Here, we need all the more to call out for God's help and wisdom, letting Him work in us. We need His help to grow, be good mentors and loving teachers, and to lay down our lives for our children. I hope this isn't sounding lofty. It's really practical. It's as easy as saying daily, "I can't do it on my own. You said You would work in me, cause me to follow You and do things Your way. Help me parent my children the way You meant me to." When we run into a situation we can't handle, instead of flying off in a panic we can pray for God's help and wisdom.

Another beautiful thing about all of this is that God will not only work in us, but as we pray and teach our children to do likewise, we can trust Him to be working in *our children* every moment of the day, whether we're there or not. It's like those commercials where someone is relaxing and they say, "I'm cleaning my oven." We can trust God to be at work in our children even when, and sometimes especially while, we aren't involved.

Showing Mercy and Being Vulnerable

One more point about "grace parenting": Anyone who is truly growing as a Christian is doing so by God's grace. And those who are growing in God's grace will tend to be merciful to others because they know it's God's grace, not their abilities, that sustains and propels them forward. (Without God's grace, I would not have made it past round fifteen of "Rick versus Rick.") We will be able to show mercy to our children because we have received mercy as children of the heavenly Father.

Don't try to be perfect. Children can see through that. Let's grow in God's grace and open the lid on our growth process to our children. Let them see our struggles and God at work helping us overcome. Let's be vulnerable, showing our weaknesses. We can ask for God's forgiveness in front of our children when we blow it. Then we can ask Him to help change and strengthen us so that we can be better parents.

In order for our children to have a successful spiritual life, a successful prayer life, and a great relationship with God, they will need to learn to rely on God's grace. They will need to ask Him to teach them and change them and, most of all, help them get to know Him. They can learn this from watching us rely on and grow in His grace as we stumble around and gradually mature as parents.

> **Let's grow in God's grace and open the lid on our growth process to our children.**

The Benefits of Imperfection

The generation of Israelites that God called stubborn and stiff-necked, the ones who died in the wilderness, raised the generation of Israelites that conquered Canaan, the Promised Land. They were perhaps the finest generation of Israelites mentioned in the Bible. That generation loved and followed God, yet they, in their turn, raised a generation that the Bible says didn't know God, were wicked, and served the idols of Canaan.

Why? Isn't the equation "godly parents = godly kids"? No. The difference is in the growth-in-grace factor. Even though the first generation was stubborn, they began to learn and change. When they made mistakes, they learned to ask God for forgiveness and help. Their children walked with them through the desert. They saw their parents' mistakes and God's miracles and punishments. They grew with their parents and grew up to serve God.

Then they got comfortable in the Promised Land. They didn't

face the same struggles and see the same miracles and direct punishments. As a result, they didn't teach their children or grow in grace with them.

If we're not perfect, we can rejoice because we're the perfect candidates to raise spiritual children. Our growing along with them is the way they'll learn to trust in God and grow in His grace.

Lincoln's Prayers

At the beginning of this section we met Abraham Lincoln, who learned that prayer was life's foundation. Reading about the life of Lincoln, you can see how he could have thought prayer was a last resort. A tall, strong young man who was extremely popular with all who got to know him; he was funny, witty, and could speak and tell stories like few others. He was a hard worker, put himself through law school, and kept going toward his goals although death, tragedy, and failure tried to diminish his drive and invite him to despair. But when he was elected president of the United States and found himself shortly thereafter responsible for leading his country through the horror of civil war, his public and private comments about prayer showed that he began to see his own wisdom and strength as grossly insufficient.

President Lincoln once said,

I was early brought up to the reflection that nothing in my power would succeed without the direct assistance of the Almighty. I have often wished that I was a more devout man than I am. Nevertheless, awed by the greatest difficulties of my Administration, when I could not see any other resort, I would place my whole reliance on God, knowing all would go well, and He would decide for the right.

Another time, he gave this reply to a doctor who attempted to thank him for the way in which the wounded soldiers were being cared for:

One rainy night I could not sleep. The wounds of the soldiers and sailors distressed me; their pains pierced my heart, and I asked God to show me how they could have better relief. After wrestling some time in prayer, He put the plans of the Sanitary Commission in my mind, and they have been carried out pretty much as God gave them to me that night.

Doctor, thank our kind Heavenly Father and not me for the Sanitary Commission.[1]

Shortly after the battle at Gettysburg had been fought, Abraham Lincoln was asked why he had been so confident about the positive outcome of the battle. After hesitating for a moment, he replied,

Well, I will tell you how it was. In the pinch of the campaign up there when everybody seemed panic stricken, and nobody could tell what was going to happen, oppressed by the gravity of our affairs, I went to my room one day, and I locked the door, and got down on my knees before Almighty God, and prayed to Him mightily for victory at Gettysburg. I told Him that this was His war, and our cause was His cause, but we couldn't stand another Fredericksburg or Chancellorsville. And I then and there made a solemn vow to the Almighty God, that if He would stand by our boys in Gettysburg, I would stand by Him. And He did stand by our boys, and I will stand by Him. And after that (I don't know how it was, and I can't explain it) soon a sweet comfort crept into my soul that God Almighty had taken the whole business into His own hands and that things would go all right at Gettysburg. And that is why I had no fears about it.[2]

Abraham Lincoln began to rely more and more on prayer and to speak about that reliance publicly. He brought the United States through one of its most difficult times, but in order to do it he had to discover that prayer is fundamental, that nothing of lasting value can be accomplished without the union of man and God through prayer.

Questions

1. What are some of your personal imperfections?

_____

_____

How can you use your struggles to overcome these imperfections to teach your children about God's grace?

_____

_____

2. What are some things that your children struggle with? Take a moment to write down some of the problems your children have talked to you about in the past week or two.

_____

_____

3. How can you use some of your past experiences to guide them through these issues?

_____

_____

Ideas for Prayer

- Thank God that you can always turn to Him for help in raising your children.
- Think of some issues or situations in your role as a parent right now that require God's guidance. Ask God to give you wisdom for how to deal with these things.
- Commit your day—your victories, failures, thoughts, words, and deeds—to God. Ask Him to use them for His glory.
- Ask God to pour out His grace on you and your children and draw you closer to Him.

Prayer for Kids

Here is a sample prayer your children can use.

"Dear Father, thank You for my mom and dad. Help me to be patient with them, and help them to be patient with me. Thank You for giving me a mom and dad who love me and help me with my problems. In Jesus' name, amen."

---

1. Emmanuel Hertz, comp., *Lincoln Talks* (New York: Halcyon, 1941), 576.
2. William J. Wolf, *The Almost Chosen People: A Study of the Religion of Abraham Lincoln,* (New York: Doubleday, 1959), 125.

PART 3

"Go!"

Through prayer and the constant reading and studying of Scripture, the minister had come to know God and His Word to a point that he confidently believed in trusting God to answer prayer. He saw God repeatedly meet his needs, direct his steps, teach him, and change him. He saw his prayers answered as he trusted and served a living and faithful God.

As he once wrote, "I judged myself bound to be the servant of the Church of Christ in the particular point on which I had obtained mercy: namely in being able to take God by His word and to rely upon it."[1]

Through his prayers, his faith grew. When others doubted, he trusted. In fact, when he counseled people in times of trouble—whether workers, businesspeople, or professionals—he always encouraged them to pray, trust God, and expect Him to act on their behalf. Often they responded with fear and doubt. He said of this, "It was evident enough that God was not looked upon by them as the *living* God. My spirit was oft times bowed down by this, and I longed to set something before the children of God, whereby they might see that He does not forsake, even in our day, those who rely upon Him."[2]

This man began talking to God about taking on a visible project so large that it would be a monument to Christians and non-Christians everywhere to the fact that God is alive and answers prayer.

He himself had no money or means by which to accomplish the task. He also committed up front that he would never let anyone but God know of the initial or ongoing needs of the project and that he would never ask anyone but God for anything. God had him move forward with the project and consistently answered his prayers.

Many, many thousands of people have heard of, read of, and been inspired to trust God by what God accomplished through George Mueller and his prayers.

Our children can grow up to have great faith. Consistent prayers help them to develop that faith as they see God alive and active in their lives. Part 3 helps you teach your children the practical, everyday elements and process of prayer. This final section will give you the hands-on suggestions, answers, and activities you'll need to help get the job done. The suggestions in this section, though, are not an attempt to put forward the ultimate system or provide an answer to every question. Every situation and child is unique, so only God can give those answers and solutions. Instead, the following can act as a help as your children grow in their relationship with and faith in God.

---

1. A. C. Brooks, comp., *Answers to Prayer: From George Mueller's Narratives* (Chicago: Moody, n.d.), 8.
2. Ibid.

Growing Up in Prayer

WE HAVE 64 QUESTIONS ABOUT PRAYER. I LEFT ROOM
BESIDE EACH ONE FOR THE ANSWER AND BIBLE VERSES.
AND COULD WE GET TEN COPIES WHEN YOU'RE DONE?

Growing Up in Prayer

Prayer does not change God, but [it] changes him who prays.
Søren Kierkegaard

A complex world cannot have simple answers. That's why debate over possible solutions is so common. American citizens, politicians, and economists disagree concerning whether a balanced budget is possible and, if so, how to reach it. Canadians argue whether predominantly French-speaking Quebec is a different culture and should be granted autonomy from Canada. And among the world of working parents, social experts debate whether spending "quality time" with children makes up for reduced "quantity time": Some family experts say yes; many say no.[1]

When it comes to teaching our children to pray, we must be cautious about saying there is one simple answer. Each prayer teaching and training process is unique. Therefore each situation has different answers, and we cannot list every one in this book. But be comforted by this: the ideas listed here come not from brilliant world leaders, scholars, child psychologists, or theologians, but from regular parents who pray and trust God for wisdom to work in "the trenches."

Thus, in this final section we will cover the basics and give you a marvelous foundation of information from which to work. However, as a parent, you are still on the hook to seek God yourself and ask for His help and wisdom in the process.

One other caution as we consider approaches in our teaching: Let's remember not to push our children. Each child is an individual, created to have an individual relationship with God, a relationship which is more important than the performance or the process. If you start out using one of the suggestions in this section and it doesn't work, simply pray and think it through until you have another. However, don't stop the training process! Remember, God is committed to helping make it work.

The process of teaching any major life skill to children is gradual.

Developing the Life Skill of Prayer

The process of teaching any major life skill to children is gradual. We start with the basics when they are young and, hopefully, end with them going into adulthood with the skills fully developed and firmly in place.

Teaching prayer is no exception. We need to start simply, teaching them prayer shortly after they "hatch" and helping them get to a fully developed and growing prayer life by the time they leave the nest. To help us stay on track with this process, we need intermediate goals along the way to the final goal. These intermediate steps can be defined as a series of prayer stages that we move our children through.

We are always mindful, of course, that the stages must not dictate the growth. Rather, evidence of growth should dictate the movement from stage to stage: Prayer is individual, and relationship with God cannot be forced.

Samuel and Jesus

We can see the typical stages in the life of Samuel, one of the greatest men in the Bible, a prophet who boldly declared God's truth and obeyed all that God commanded him to do. He was also a great child. In fact, Samuel's is one of the few childhoods described in the Bible. Another childhood we have some description of is Jesus'—and it's interesting to note the parallels between the two.

1. Hannah gave Samuel to God before he was born, to be raised by God in His house and for His benefit. Before Jesus was born, God gave Him to us, via Mary, to be raised by us in our world and for our benefit.

2. When Samuel was born, his mother Hannah sang a song of praise to God. When Mary was pregnant with Jesus, she sang a song of praise similar to Hannah's. Mary even seemed to borrow and quote from Hannah's song.

3. Both boys found favor with and wisdom from God. Compare 1 Samuel 2:26 and Luke 2:52.

4. Both found their spiritual turning points as children. When Samuel was about twelve, God spoke to him in the temple. This was a turning point in his relationship with God. When Jesus was twelve, His three-day stay in the temple seemed to mark a turning point in His relationship with God. When His parents finally found Him and Mary questioned Him, Jesus answered, "Why were you searching for me? . . . Didn't you know I had to be in *my Father's* house?" (Luke 2:49, italics added). Although Jesus continued to be obedient, a switch in focus had taken place from His parents to God.

It seems that Mary needed a model for bringing up God's Son so that God could bring about what He had promised to Abraham. That model was Samuel. He can be ours too.

The "Samuel Stages"

Samuel's childhood is recorded in such a way that the Bible gives us six reports about him at different stages of growth, physically and in his relationship to God. These six "Samuel Stages" can be used as a guide to help us take our children from birth to spiritual maturity. Since they suggest that a progressive pattern exists for our own children's prayer development, our teaching about prayer should be sensitive to our children's stage of development.

But first, we need to follow Hannah's example and give our children to God for their whole lives. We can't make that decision for them, but we can make it for ourselves by dedicating them to God. Such dedication (at any age) is not just saying a prayer. It is committing to learn and do everything we can, all our lives, to teach and train them to follow God. It means committing (with God's strength and help) to teach them to lead a Christ-centered life and to help them develop a relationship with God.

1. Love and Nurture (1 Samuel 1:10–23)

Samuel Stage One is love and nurture and covers birth to approximately age three. Hannah kept Samuel home until he was weaned. In those days in the Middle East, weaning took place at about three years or older. (The practical reason was the difficulty of keeping other milk fresh in the heat.)

The first three years are a gentle, nurturing process. Don't send your child to God alone. Feed and nourish him.

Following in Hannah's footsteps, spiritually speaking, the first three years are a gentle, nurturing process. Don't send your child to God alone. Feed and nourish him. From the time you know your child has been conceived until he is at least three, pray your prayers for him on your own but also pray over him simple, short prayers that affirm God's love and care for him. Also, begin giving him simple biblical truth, "the pure milk of the word,"[2] on a regular basis. That includes the following: (1) God loves you; (2) God made everything; (3) God takes care of us; and (4) prayer is talking to God.

Reflections

Take a moment to brainstorm some ways you can affirm these four truths to your children (regardless of their "stage"). How can you show or remind them of God's love? His power and interest? His desire for relationship with your children?

_____

_____

_____

_____

_____

2. Involvement (1 Samuel 1:24–28)

After Samuel was weaned, Hannah took him to the temple to live there:

> "So now I give him to the LORD. For his whole life he will be given over to the LORD." And he worshiped the LORD there. (1 Samuel 1:28)

Although Hannah's methods are a little drastic, the point is that she took Samuel to God.

In Samuel Stage Two, from about the age of four to age six, we need to actively take our children to God and help them become committed to Him.

During the first part of this stage, at bedtime or any time they have a need, we should either pray over our children (with their understanding that these are their prayers we're helping them with) or have them repeat a simple prayer after us. By the end of the stage, they should be able to say basic prayers alone.

When making a transition from one way of praying with your child to another, always do so gradually. Make sure she is excited about growing up and moving to the next stage. Let her know where you're going and why, and then move there progressively. For example, when it's time to move your child from your saying her prayers, as she listens, to her repeating what you say, or from repeated prayers to saying her own prayers, try alternating nights for a while.

To start involving your child in the prayer process, first discuss what he would like to pray about. Ask for his input and give suggestions regarding events from his day or things he is currently interested in: an upcoming special occasion, a need or desire, a friend or family member who needs prayer, or thankyous for things that happened that day. This process helps your child begin to understand what and how to pray, but, more importantly, it heads him in the direction of acknowledging God in everything and learning to rely on Him.

The main thing you need to teach your children during this time is God's place in their lives and the place and purpose of prayer. They should begin to understand that prayer is for every day, it's important for all of life, and it's God's way of letting them get to know Him and receive His help and care. Here are five great truths to establish your child in during this stage:

1. God hears us when we pray.
2. God wants to be our friend.
3. God wants us to talk to Him every day about everything we're thinking about and need.
4. Prayer is great and really important.
5. God wants us to pray for others.

As you teach these important truths during this stage, relax and have a little fun. Be brief. Pray about what the child is interested in. Present, but do not push, the serious side of things. If your child squirms around, opens her eyes, or interrupts during prayer, lovingly encourage her toward concentration. Don't get uptight about the outward distractions.

3. God's Care (1 Samuel 2:18–21)
In the third report about Samuel's childhood, we see him well provided for and wearing priestly garments that his mother made and brought to him each year. The priests were not given land of their own to work and live off. God was to be their portion or provision. However, the verses preceding this report on Samuel's growth describe Eli's wicked sons. Instead of trusting God to provide for them, they were looking out for themselves by breaking God's law and stealing from God's people.

The end of this report on Samuel says, "The boy Samuel grew up in the presence of the LORD" (1 Samuel 2:21). Samuel was learning that God cared for him and would look after him. Your child needs to know that when she grows up in God's presence and stays there, He will take care of her, meet her needs, and answer her prayers. The Bible says that we can love God because He first loved us.

In Samuel Stage Three, children between ages seven to nine should have God's love, care, and provision reinforced and made real. This is when they need to hear your faith stories and start collecting their own. Prayer needs to become a concrete way to receive specific answers and help. At this stage, your child should be saying his own prayers, with you alongside to coach, help, and encourage. He should be thinking of what he wants and needs and learning to ask God for help and provision.

These two suggestions will help you help your child pray. First, "Ping-Pong" prayers. Your daughter says a prayer of her own, you say a prayer for her, she says a prayer of her own, and so on. Second, expand the discussions about what needs to be prayed about (begun in stage two). Sit with your child and talk through her day. Uncover her concerns and discuss events coming up and the needs of those around her until you have a short prayer list. Then have her pray for those things.

Children between ages seven to nine should have God's love, care, and provision reinforced and made real.

This is the stage in which you need to start teaching your child to actively trust God. This should be done by affirming God's love, character, and willingness to care for him. Choosing some appropriate memory verses to go over together each night will help in this process. (For example, see Psalm 37:4; Isaiah 26:3; John 16:24.) Also, help him recognize God's answers and compile his faith stories, thereby strengthening his faith.

4. Personal Growth (1 Samuel 2:22–26)

In 1 Samuel 2:22–25 we read of Eli confronting his sons about their actions and the bad things being said about them. But they do not listen. In contrast, Samuel has a healthy report of personal growth: "And the boy Samuel continued to grow in stature and in favor with the LORD and with men" (verse 26).

In Samuel Stage Four (approximately ages ten and eleven), our children should be learning to pray and be submitting themselves and their behavior to God. They need to learn that God wants to give them wisdom, work with and inside them, and help them to be all they can be. At this stage, you will need to help your children learn to pray about who they are. This is a crucial time for them to learn what the Bible says about how we should act and behave—what God expects of us.

During this stage, your child should be heading toward praying on his own. You still need to be there to help him be consistent and to help when necessary. But you should be doing so only occasionally, typically early in this stage, for variety and assistance.

In stage four, it is still important to sit by the child's bedside and talk with him about prayer. Let him know how your prayer life

This is a crucial time for children to learn what the Bible says about how we should act and behave.

and personal growth are going; talk to him about something you've learned or are learning; ask him what's going on in his life. You may suggest that your son pray about certain things and suggest how to do that. When he begins to pray on his own, at first he may want you to sit and listen. Or he may want to have you hear the basics and then pray a few things silently. That's good. He's learning to be personal with God and talk to Him about things that he may not be willing to talk about with anyone else. Eventually, he will want you to leave after your nightly conversation so he can pray on his own.

In this stage, help your child see the growth in himself. Never say critically, "You better pray about improving that character flaw (or bad habit or mistake)." Lovingly encourage him and tell him the good things you see in his character and praise him for growth. Be careful not to just send him to bed to pray on his own. By this stage, bedtime prayer has become a wonderful together time for you and him. Abandoning that so he can grow in prayer could backfire.

Reflections

Write down some good things you see in each of your children that you can encourage them with. What areas have you seen them growing in? Share these with them.

_____

_____

_____

5. Relationship, Direction, and Obedience (1 Samuel 2:27–3:18)

In this report, an unnamed prophet pronounced God's judgment on Eli's sons for their behavior in the temple and on Eli for not doing anything about it. The bottom line was that they spurned the opportunity to be in God's presence and get to know Him. They didn't value or follow God's calling and direction for their lives and they consistently disobeyed God by doing what they knew was wrong.

Another growth report on Samuel follows (3:1–18). It tells how the boy Samuel heard God calling his name. Three times Samuel thought it was Eli and three times he went to see what Eli wanted. The third time Eli clued in and told Samuel, if the voice called him again, to say, "Speak, LORD, for your servant is listening" (verse 9). Samuel did just that, and God told him what would happen to Eli and his sons. In the morning Samuel went about his duties. When Eli demanded to hear what God had said, Samuel told him everything, even though he was afraid.

The contrast is simple. Unlike Eli's own sons, Samuel valued his opportunity to get to know God and be in His presence. He was willing to follow God's direction and calling for his life, and he began to practice obedience.

The report on Samuel ends with these words (which also take him and us through to Samuel Stage Six, spiritual maturity):

> The LORD was with Samuel as he grew up, and he let none of his words fall to the ground. And all Israel from Dan to Beersheba recognized that Samuel was attested as a prophet of the LORD. The LORD continued to appear at Shiloh, and there he revealed himself to Samuel through his word. And Samuel's word came to all Israel (1 Samuel 3:19—4:1).

Once our children hit their teenage years, the three things they need to be learning more about and focusing on in their prayer life are:

1. Seeking God, asking Him to help them get to know Him and His Word, and developing a deeper relationship with Him;

2. Giving their life to God, asking Him for wisdom and direction for what He has for them (both ultimately and in the smaller "today" decisions); and

3. Praying about and trusting God to work in them to help them be obedient and follow Him in everything.

Although the idea and practice of praying throughout the day should be developed through all the stages, such prayer becomes key during stage five. If your young teenagers haven't learned to talk to God on the spot about whatever concerns them, bedtime prayers, and therefore prayer itself, will start to become less important to them. It's almost impossible to pass the day without a thought for God and then wholeheartedly turn everything over to Him at night. Because relationship with God should be the foundation of our lives, everything should be set on and flow out of that foundation. For our children, then, bedtime should no longer be the primary training field. Life itself—every day, every minute—should become the primary place for you to help and guide them.

6. Spiritual Maturity (1 Samuel 3:20–21)

This final report on Samuel's life takes him into adulthood and spiritual maturity. Samuel is no longer in the temple, relating only to Eli and his parents. He's now living his life in the community of Israel. "And all Israel from Dan to Beersheba recognized that Samuel was attested as a prophet of the LORD. . . . And Samuel's word came to all Israel" (1 Samuel 3:20, 4:1).

In this final stage, our children are reaching toward spiritual maturity; that is, walking in God's will and calling, and having a wonderful relationship with God and a life that counts.

When life, and specifically your child's life, provides you with a chalkboard and a good size piece of chalk, pick it up and help her by reinforcing her life with encouraging truths. Take that opportunity to talk together (like you did earlier, during her bedtime) and help direct your child godward with encouragement, faith stories, and an offer to help and pray.

If our children go through the first "Samuel Stages," they'll have what they need to go through stage five and stage six. They will know that God loves them and wants the best for them; that He created them uniquely and has a special job for them; that He will care for them, provide for them, and answer their prayers. They will have the confidence that they can change, learn, grow in Christ, and be all that God has made them to be. In short, when we build in stages, we end up with a foundation that is built for and leads to the final stage of spiritual maturity.

It's probable that many who read this book will have children who, age wise, should be in a different stage than they're in. That's okay. The key is in the stages, not the ages. If I look at the process of how and when I learned to pray, I can see the stages even though I went through them as a young adult:

1. Knowing that God loves me.
2. Learning that I need to pray and learning to pray.
3. Learning to receive God's love, having Him meet my needs and answer my prayers.
4. Learning that God wants me to be like Him and that He'll help me change and grow.
5. Starting to develop a relationship with God. Learning He has a plan for me and asking Him for His will.
6. Learning to be obedient to His Word and leading.

The process flows from a gradual introduction to God's love, through to obedience, relationship, and following His will for our lives. No matter what the ages of your children, start with God's love and work up from there. Older children probably will move through the process more quickly. But remember to watch and see where they are and what God is doing with them. You can't push growth with stages. You must watch the growth and move the stages around them.

No matter what the ages of your children, start with God's love and work up from there.

If you start your child at an older age, you may not want to follow all the instructions I've laid out for praying with her. Your fourteen-year-old may not appreciate the idea of "Ping-Pong" prayers, for instance. She might want you to pray with her, though, or listen to you pray, or just sit down and talk to you about it. She may want to read this book for herself. And remember, with teens especially, don't push. God doesn't push. He draws people lovingly to Himself only as fast as they respond. The best thing you can do is let your teen see some "stage four" happening in your own personal growth that is leading you to serve, love, and encourage her.

The wages of sin is death, but the "Stages of Samuel" will lead your child to life!

Activity: Stages and Prayer

Write down the name of each of your children on the top of a piece of paper. Then write what Samuel Stage you think each is at. In their present stage, what does each one need to know about prayer? About God? What are some ways you can teach them these things?

_____

_____

_____

_____

_____

Question

How does the stage your children are at compare to where you would like them to be?

_____

_____

_____

Write down five things that you can do to help each child move forward to the next level.

_____

_____

_____

_____

_____

Ideas for Prayer

- Thank God that you and your children can grow closer to Him each day through prayer.
- Ask God to show you what you need to do to help bring your children to spiritual maturity.
- Ask God to increase your children's faith and to build a desire in them to know Him more.

Prayer for Kids

Here is a sample prayer your children can use.

"Dear heavenly Father, I want to know You better. Please show me how I can learn more about You. Help me to spend more time talking to You in prayer. In Jesus' name, amen."

_____

1. In its cover story, "The Myth of Quality Time," *Newsweek* magazine makes a case that two full-time working parents cannot give adequate attention to their children by having limited, yet quality, time with them. See Laura Shapiro, "The Myth of Quality Time," *Newsweek,* 12 May 1997, 62–68.
2. See 1 Peter 2:2 NASB.

Introducing Your Child to God

OUR FATHER IN HEAVEN, HAROLD BE YOUR NAME...

Introducing Your Child to God

If our experience is not what God wants it to be, it is because of our unbelief in the love of God, in the power of God, and in the reality of God's promises.

Andrew Murray

Here are two renditions of a portion of the Lord's Prayer (Matthew 6:9–13) with very different perspectives on who God is. They illustrate that how we pray and what we expect from our relationship with God reflect who we—and our children—believe God is.

"Our perfect, loving Father, who is in heaven—a beautiful place that reflects Your character, full of happiness, without sadness or evil. May Your name be honored because You are so great that everyone should know You. Let Your perfect kingdom, full of right and happiness, come here on earth and set people free to be with You and be loved by You. Let Your will for the perfect peace, happiness, and fulfillment of Your people be done here on earth just like it is in heaven—where Your people are like You, love each other perfectly, and enjoy everything You've made for them. Please meet our needs today as You always do so wonderfully.

Forgive our mistakes and imperfections as we receive Your grace to grow, and as we love and forgive the people You've so wonderfully placed in our lives. . . ."

"Our all-seeing Father, far away in heaven. Holy and beyond what we can understand or relate to is Your name. Your Kingdom come, to squash all who refuse to obey You. Your will be imposed on everyone, like it is in heaven, where everyone finally has to be perfect. Please give us some bread today, so we don't starve. (I don't want to bother You with more than that.) Please forgive me my sins (don't let me end up in the hot place) as I forgive the rotten sinners around me. . . ."

Children need to have a basic knowledge of who God is, beginning when they can understand what we are saying.

We *must* teach our children who God is, what He's like, and what He is willing to do for them. If they don't believe God loves them or they get the idea He is always judging them to see if they measure up, the mechanics of prayer will not matter; the relationship and results won't come. We need to teach them who God is and that He acts according to His character.

God created us to be in relationship with Him. When our children really understand who God is and what He's willing to do for them, they won't have a problem building a relationship with Him and getting their prayers answered.

Following are five important realities about God you can teach your children to enhance their prayer lives. With them are simple definitions, suggestions on how to teach, and some verses you can read to or memorize with them.

1. God Is the One, Eternal Creator

Some of the most common questions children ask about God are: Who made God? Where did God come from? What does God look like? Does He have any friends or is He the only one?

Children need to have a basic knowledge of who God is, beginning when they can understand what we are saying. Here are the basics:

- God created everything we can and can't see.
- There is only one God. He can do anything. He is every-where and knows everything.
- God was not created or born. He has always been. God invented time, the art of creating, birth, beginnings, and endings. We think that everything has to start and end because that's how God made the world to work, but He is bigger than the things He made.

Suggestions

When explaining who God is to our children, it is important to help them understand that some things about God are beyond our ability to comprehend. We can use allegories to explain some of God's attributes such as that He always exists, knows every-thing, is everywhere, and can do anything.

I like to compare our trying to understand God to two pet hamsters. They are in a glass cage arguing over whether the stuff they see outside the cage really exists. Because they can't get through the invisible wall, they conclude that it does not—it is just a picture of some kind. They have neither all the information nor the ability to understand the information if they did have it. But that doesn't mean nothing outside the cage exists. (You can adjust this allegory to match pets and/or animals that your child has or can identify with.)

When it comes to helping our kids understand how God can be everywhere at once, know everything that is going on every-where, and even hear everyone's prayers at once, take them to the confined hamsters. God created our children's marvelous yet lim-ited brains. He also created the idea of being in one place at a time and limitations. The Bible tells us that God is everywhere and knows everything. Nothing is impossible to Him. When He created you, He put you in one place, knowing only what you've learned, and only being able to do a limited number of things. It is silly then for us to look at ourselves and say it's impossible for God to be without limits, because we have limits.

In terms of our children's understanding—and our own—we can be compared to the hamsters in the cage trying to grasp the mysteries of the universe beyond. The Bible tells us that we can't even imagine what He has prepared for us after we leave this world. For now God has chosen to limit us. We should not use those limits to define and understand God.

Key Verses

Here are key verses your child can read (and memorize). They show God is present everywhere; He is all-powerful; and He is all-knowing.

> Where can I go from your Spirit? Where can I flee from your presence? If I go up to the heavens, you are there; if I make my bed in the depths, you are there. If I rise on the wings of the dawn, if I settle on the far side of the sea, even there your hand will guide me, your right hand will hold me fast. (Psalm 139:7–10; see also Jeremiah 23:23–24)

> Ah, Sovereign Lord, you have made the heavens and the earth by your great power and outstretched arm. Nothing is too hard for you. (Jeremiah 32:17; see also Job 42:2 and Luke 1:37)

> Great is our Lord and mighty in power; his understanding has no limit. (Psalm 147:5; see also Psalm 44:21 and Isaiah 46:10)

Responding to Their Creator

The three elements—God as the one true God, the Creator, the eternal God—form a basic introduction to God. Such an introduction should also include a personal introduction to a relationship with Him through Jesus. Children can respond to an opportunity or ask to accept Jesus as early as three years old. Here's a little instruction to assist you in introducing your child to God.

1. Read her a good storybook of the life, death, and resurrection of Jesus. If your child is older, have her read the gospel of John.

2. Read her John 3:16 and then explain that none of us is perfect—we have all done things wrong. "That's called sin and sin keeps us from being God's children. The punishment for sin is dying and being apart from God. But God sent His own Son Jesus to die on the cross for our sins. He took our place. So, if we ask God to forgive us because of what Jesus did for us, He will. He'll make us His children."

3. Ask her if she wants to pray and ask God to forgive her and make her His child right now. By saying "right now," if the time isn't right, you leave the door open for next time. If the answer is no, read your child the story again at another time. God will work in her heart. If the answer is yes, have her repeat this simple prayer: "Dear God, I know I've made wrong choices and done bad things. I'm sorry. I know Jesus died for my sins and rose from the dead. I know He is Lord of everything. Please forgive me, God. Help me trust and obey You and make right choices. Thank You for loving me and making me Your child. In Jesus' name, amen."

Children can respond to an opportunity or ask to accept Jesus as early as three years old.

Then get excited with your daughter (or son). "In the same way, I tell you, there is rejoicing in the presence of the angels of God over one sinner who repents" (Luke 15:10). All heaven throws a party. You can too. Have a "spiritual birthday" party for your child—who has now become a child of God (John 1:12).

Reflections

1. Why is teaching your children that God is their Creator so important?

_____

_____

_____

2. How does this fact impact their daily lives?

_____

_____

_____

2. God Loves You

The well-known Scripture verse John 3:16 begins "For God so loved the world that he gave . . ." The result of love, its corresponding action, is giving. Significantly, the apostle Paul said the God of love desires to give: "He who did not spare his own Son, but gave him up for us all—how will he not also, along with him, graciously give us all things?" (Romans 8:32). When we teach our children that God is love and loves them, we need to help them understand that doesn't just mean that God has a warm, fuzzy feeling for them: He gives. And He wants them to give too, just as His Son gave (1 John 3:16–18).

> **The result of love, its corresponding action, is giving.**

Our children need to learn that the God who is love, who loves them more than they can even imagine, will not sit back and refuse to act on their behalf. When God says, "I love you," the word love is a very active verb.

Suggestions

Always affirm God's love for your child. Before and/or after prayer, tell him that God loves him. Then tell him something God does because He loves him (try to make your affirmation correspond to something your child is currently praying about):

"God loves you and He hears and answers your prayers. He knows you want a bicycle."

"God loves you and He likes to help you with problems you might have like your friend's rudeness to you today."

"God loves you and wants you to have a happy life."

To reinforce that love is a verb, start having "love-surprise" days in your home. A love-surprise is an unexpected gift presented to a family member in love. Take a week or a day for each member of your family. In the allotted time period, each of the other family members has to think of and execute a love-surprise for that person. Your younger ones may need help. This activity not only can be used to reinforce how love requires corresponding action but will help your children experience firsthand the joy of showing their love and having others demonstrate it to them.

The Bible says that God does for us exceedingly above and beyond what we can ask or think. Often when He answers prayer He blows us away. When this happens we can call it a love-surprise from God.

Key Verses
This verse focuses on the great love God has for us:

> How great is the love the Father has lavished on us, that we should be called children of God! And that is what we are! (1 John 3:1; see also Romans 8:32 and 1 John 4:16)

3. God Is Merciful and Full of Grace

Grace is unmerited action on behalf of another. When we say God is full of grace, we are saying that He will answer us and meet our needs even though He doesn't have to and we don't deserve it. He does it because He loves us, He wants to, and it is His character to do so. In His mercy He will not give us what our sins deserve. Because of such compassion, we can "approach the throne of grace with confidence, so that we may receive mercy and find grace to help us in our time of need" (Hebrews 4:16).

Grace is a necessary attribute of God to teach anyone who wants to grow in relationship with Him and receive answers to their prayers. Often we can get the idea that God hears us because we've been good or we are one of His favorites. Or the reverse: We have trouble asking or trusting God for something because we haven't been as good as we should be or we think God isn't happy with us. Although God encourages us all toward perfection and a life of good works, in Christ He is our partner, not our judge sitting at the end of the race with a stopwatch and evaluation sheet.

When we or our children go to God and pray, asking Him for anything, we are not to ask according to our good works or based on whether we deserve His answer. God set it up this way because He wants to hear and answer our prayers at every stage of our growth, no matter where we find ourselves or how our performance stacks up. His answer is dependent on His mercy and grace, not our performance; therefore, we can always come to Him with confidence and receive His help! We deserve nothing but God desires to give mercy to those who ask. Hebrews 4:16 says that we can "approach the throne of grace *with confidence*, so that we may *receive mercy*" (italics added).

When our children understand this, God can be more easily received as someone lovingly helping them grow into all He created them to be, not someone who demands performance and judges every step.

Suggestions

Have a "mercy" day. Choose a day and explain to your children what "mercy" is. Let them know that for a whole day nothing will be done on the merit/demerit system but according to mercy. This is fun because it goes both ways. Everyone is required to act according to mercy. In other words, when one of your children makes a request of you (within reason, of course) your answer is based only on two things: (1) Do I have the ability to meet the request? and (2) Is it a good thing for him or her? Whether the child deserves it or not cannot play a part; whether she has her homework done yet or her room clean does not matter. On the flip side, if you ask your children to do something for you, no excuses can escape their lips. No merit/demerit comments like, "I did it last time" or "It's not my turn" or "I really hate doing that." Just, "Okay."

It applies to siblings too. They might bombard each other with "be my slave" requests at first, but it'll balance out. Each request must be started with the words, "I appeal to your mercy."

This is a good exercise to help your children remember God's mercy, but it will also help them learn to be merciful to others, which God requires. Imagine your family all doing things for each other out of love and because they choose to be merciful!

Key Verses

Here are great verses that remind us of God's mercy:

Be merciful, just as your Father is merciful. (Luke 6:36; see also Hebrews 4:16)

Give ear, O God, and hear; open your eyes and see the desolation of the city that bears your Name. We do not make requests of you because we are righteous, but because of your great mercy. (Daniel 9:18)

4. God Is Faithful

People who are faithful are steadfast, trustworthy, and reliable. They can be counted on to do what they say. When the Bible talks about God as faithful, it emphasizes the complete dependability of His character and promises: God can be relied on to carry out His commitments to us in Christ.

When we go to God and make a request, we need to know that He is faithful and believe that He will work things out. We should not send our children to God with the idea that God may or may not answer their prayers. That is not faithfulness. Indeed, when we ask in doubt, we should not expect an answer.

When we go to God and make a request, we need to know that He is faithful and believe that He will work things out.

If any of you lacks wisdom, he should ask God, who gives generously to all without finding fault, and it will be given to him. But when he asks, he must believe and not doubt, because he who doubts is like a wave of the sea, blown and tossed by the wind. That man should not think he will receive anything from the Lord; he is a double-minded man, unstable in all he does. (James 1:5–8)

James warns against doubting. He basically says, "Don't let someone who thinks prayer is a lottery (so he might not get anything) think that he will get something." Why? Because he won't! His doubt determines it. If we let our children think that God may or may not answer their prayers, He won't, and they'll get discouraged. Our children must know that God is faithful. He can and should be depended on.

Are there times God says no? Yes. Are there times we don't know what the answer is going to be? Yes. Are there times that we know the answer is yes? Yes, there are. So how can we teach our children the difference?

Suggestions

Here are two types of prayers you can teach your children to pray and one you can teach them not to pray:

1. *No prayers.* This is the type of prayer you need to teach your children not to pray. God has already told us in the Bible that there are things for which we cannot pray. We can't pray anything contrary to His will and character. So praying that God would teach someone a lesson because your child is upset with the person, or any similar prayer, is out. Also, praying in a way that is not yielding to God's will or trusting His care is also out. (See James 4:1–3; 1 John 5:14–15.)

2. *Yes prayers.* These are prayers in which we ask God to do things He has already said He would do. These are not to be confused with "Pick-a-Promise-and-Demand-Delivery" prayers. "Pick-a-Promise-and-Demand-Delivery" assumes automatic delivery because God promised and now it's our right and His obligation. The problem is that this ignores the context of our relationship and His mercy.

   Here's the difference: You are committed to feeding your children, and they know it. Out of your love you put effort into the process. How would it feel if your children walked in five minutes before mealtime and said, "Hey, where's my supper? You're legally required to feed me and I'm hungry now!" then they ignore you during the meal and leave without a thank-you? Your kids would probably get a bowl of instant porridge for their next meal. Yes, you're committed to feeding them, but you do a nice job of it because you love them and want to see them healthy and happy. You would also like the process to enhance your relationship with them. Having them be thankful and appreciative, as opposed to demanding, helps the process.

   Yes, we can count on "yes prayers" and we need to teach our kids to count on God's faithfulness—which flows out of His love and mercy and is received in the context of a growing relationship. Otherwise, God would have just made everything automatic. Prayer is the developing of a relationship, not a vending machine.

   There are some things that God, out of His love, mercy,

and grace, has already told us we can ask for and has promised to give us. They range from wisdom (James 1:5) and Christian growth and development (1 Corinthians 1:8–9; 1 Thessalonians 5:23–24) to help with temptation (1 Corinthians 10:13) and protection from the Evil One (2 Thessalonians 3:3).

The entire New Testament should be read as a document of God's grace and intention. When you read God's announced intention—His will—anywhere in those pages, it becomes subject matter for "yes prayers." Thus, everything God requires of us become "yes prayers": help me give; help me love; help me walk in peace with my friends, my coworkers, the kids at school; help me be patient and kind; please fit me into a local church. All these are "yes prayers" because they correspond with what God has revealed in the Bible as His will.

A lot of "yes prayers" can be prayed for repeatedly because, like gaining God's wisdom, it's an ongoing process. The most important thing is that your children know God will answer their prayer at the right time, although perhaps in a different way than they might think. He is faithful and He will do it.

Prayer is the developing of a relationship, not a vending machine.

3. *Maybe prayers.* These are prayers that are OK to ask God, yet they are so specific to us that the Bible doesn't cover the issue. What about those "Ask anything and it will be given to you" Scriptures? Don't they cover maybe prayers? Maybe! Or, more specifically, yes and no.

All of the "ask anything" Scriptures are qualified by the context of their surrounding verses and by the Scriptures on the same topic. No verse of Scripture should ever be considered in isolation. For example, John chapters 14–16 center around the new relationship that all believers in Christ would have with the Father, Son, and Holy Spirit. The keys to the relationship are the receiving of God's love, grace, Spirit, direction, provision, and fellowship with God through prayer and His Spirit working in us. Also involved are the Christians' new lives of submission to God's will, trusting in His care and obeying His commands. "You did not choose me, but I chose you and appointed you to go and bear fruit—fruit that will last. Then the Father will give you whatever you ask in my name. This is my command: Love each other" (John 15:16–17).

In other words, the "ask anything" Scriptures are in the context of submitting ourselves and our lives to God's care and commands, trusting His love and allowing Him to be our Father. "This is the confidence we have in approaching God: that *if we ask anything according to his will*, he hears us. And if we know that he hears us—whatever we ask—we know that we have what we asked of him" (1 John 5:14–15, italics added). John's qualification is that "we ask anything according to his will." These verses, of course, cover "yes prayers," but they also cover "maybe prayers." The "ask anything" Scriptures outline God's desire for us to trust Him and talk to Him about everything. They also show that His intent is to say yes and make His decision according to what is best for us. But sometimes what's best for us is not what we are asking.

"Ask anything" Scriptures are in the context of submitting ourselves and our lives to God's care and commands.

Any prayer that we have should be submitted to God. We need to trust Him and His wisdom. Things work out a lot better that way because, like ourselves, He wants the best for us, but unlike ourselves He truly knows what is best. "Maybe prayers" for kids can cover some new thing they want, a part they would like in the school or church play, lessons they would like to start, or a camp they would like to go to.

Have your child talk with God, letting Him know how he is feeling, what he is thinking, and what he would like. Then have him tell God he wants Him to decide what's best and that he trusts God to work it out. Your child can also ask God for wisdom in making decisions if that's applicable. With a "maybe prayer," your child knows that God will help direct him and work things out for the best, no matter how He does it.

Key Verses
The following key verses show we can have faith in a faithful God:

> The LORD is faithful to all his promises and loving toward all he has made. (Psalm 145:13)

> Let us hold unswervingly to the hope we profess, for he who promised is faithful. (Hebrews 10:23; see also Hebrews 11:1)

5. God Is Trustworthy

When we trust someone, we know their character well enough to know that they are trustworthy. Perhaps one of the highest relational compliments is, "I trust you." Whereas faithfulness has to do with performance, trustworthiness seems more to do with character. God's character is completely trustworthy. We can put our whole lives, everything we believe and hold dear, into His hands and know that He won't let us down in any way.

We need to teach our children to do exactly that: Put everything, past, present, and future into God's hands, including who you are as a person. We should encourage them daily to pray, "God, I trust you with everything. Please make me who You want me to be and take me where You want me to go."

When we teach our children that God is trustworthy and help them to trust Him completely, God's joy and peace will fill them so that they will overflow with hope (Romans 15:13). Trusting God, His character, and therefore His overall care and custodianship of our lives, is absolutely foundational to a relationship with Him. Such trust will sustain our children as they await the outcome of "maybe prayers."

Suggestions
Write out the key verses on the next page (or any other simple verses you can find on the trustworthiness of God) and put them on your refrigerator. Read them to your children each morning as part of your daily routine and talk together about what the verses mean. Doing this will help remind you that God is still on the job—and after a while you'll find your family has memorized the verses!

Key Verses

Here are three key Scripture passages:

> Do not let your hearts be troubled. Trust in God; trust also in me. (John 14:1)

> Anyone who trusts in him will never be put to shame. (Romans 10:11)

> Trust in the LORD with all your heart and lean not on your own understanding; in all your ways acknowledge him, and he will make your paths straight. (Proverbs 3:5–6)

Reflections

1. Think about some recent incidents when you've taught your children about God. What elements of God's character do you tend to stress the most? His grace, His love, His justice?

_____

_____

_____

2. What elements of His character could receive more emphasis in your teaching? How could you do that?

_____

_____

_____

In conclusion, tell your child, "God is good. He can blow you away with His love and faithfulness." The following verse can increase your children's (and your) hope and excitement as they watch God work in their lives: "Now to him who is able to do immeasurably more than all we ask or imagine, according to his power that is at work within us" (Ephesians 3:20). Write that verse on a card and hang it on the refrigerator. When your children read it, the verse just may blow them away!

Activity: Trust Treasure Chest

Build a "Trust Treasure Chest." Sit down with your children and decorate a shoe box like a treasure chest. Put a sign on it that says, "Trust Treasure Chest." Put out pens and small pieces of paper. Divide into two teams and have a contest to see who can write out the greatest number of things you can put into God's hands and trust Him with. (Of course, every entry is admissible.) Later, when one of your children is concerned about something, write it on a piece of paper at prayer time, pray about it together, and have him or her go put it into the Trust Treasure Chest. When your children get concerned about that issue again, remind them where it is, encourage them to keep trusting God, and pray with them, thanking God for His trustworthiness.

Questions

1. Where do you usually look for answers to your children's questions about God and prayer?

_____

_____

_____

2. Take a moment to think about the ten questions about God that you are most asked by your children. Write them down.

_____

_____

_____

_____

_____

_____

_____

In addition to this book, the following resources can help provide you with answers to your questions. Look for them in your church library or your local Christian bookstore.

For Children:

Bowler, K. Christie. *The Amazing Treasure Bible Storybook.* Grand Rapids, MI: Zondervan, 1997. (Ages 8–12)

Osborne, Rick, with Ed Strauss and Kevin Miller. *Kidcordance.* Grand Rapids, MI: Zonderkidz, 1999. (Ages 8–12)

Osborne, Rick, with K. Christie Bowler. *I Want to Know About the Bible.* Grand Rapids, MI: Zondervan, 1998. (Ages 8–12)

———. *I Want to Know About God.* Grand Rapids, MI: Zondervan, 1998. (Ages 8–12)

———. *I Want to Know About Jesus.* Grand Rapids, MI: Zondervan, 1998. (Ages 8–12)

———. *I Want to Know About Prayer.* Grand Rapids, MI: Zondervan, 1998. (Ages 8–12)

———. *I Want to Know About the Church.* Grand Rapids, MI: Zondervan, 1998. (Ages 8–12)

———. *I Want to Know About the Holy Spirit.* Grand Rapids, MI: Zondervan, 1998. (Ages 8–12)

———. *I Want to Know About the Ten Commandments.* Grand Rapids, MI: Zonderkidz, 1998. (Ages 8–12)

———. *I Want to Know About the Fruit of the Spirit.* Grand Rapids, MI: Zonderkidz, 1999. (Ages 8–12)

Osborne, Rick, and Elaine Osborne. *The Singing Bible.* Wheaton, IL: Tyndale, 2000. (Audiotape; ages 2–7)

van der Maas, Ed M. *Adventure Bible Handbook.* Grand Rapids, MI: Zondervan, 1994. (Ages 8–14)

The NirV Kids' Quest Study Bible. Grand Rapids, MI: Zondervan, 1998.

For Parents:

Burkett, Larry, and Rick Osborne. *Financial Parenting.* Colorado Springs, CO: Chariot, 1996.

———. *Your Child Wonderfully Made.* Chicago, IL: Moody, 1998.

Lucas, Daryl J., gen. ed. *105 Questions Children Ask About Money Matters.* Wheaton, IL: Tyndale, 1997.

Osborne, Rick. *Talking to Your Children About God.* New York: HarperSanFrancisco, 1998.

———. *Teaching Your Children How to Pray*. Chicago, IL: Moody, 2000.

Osborne, Rick with K. Christie Bowler. *Your Child and the Christian Life*. Chicago, IL: Moody, 1998.

Osborne, Rick with Kevin Miller. *Your Child and the Bible*. Chicago, IL: Moody, 1998.

———. *Your Child and the Jesus*. Chicago, IL: Moody, 1999.

Trent, John, Rick Osborne, and Kurt Bruner, gen. eds. *Parents' Guide to the Spiritual Growth of Children*. Wheaton, IL: Tyndale, 2000.

Veerman, David R. et al. *101 Questions Children Ask About God*. Wheaton, IL: Tyndale, 1992.

———. *102 Questions Children Ask About the Bible*. Wheaton, IL: Tyndale, 1994.

———. *103 Questions Children Ask About Right from Wrong*. Wheaton, IL: Tyndale, 1995.

———. *104 Questions Children Ask About Heaven and Angels*. Wheaton, IL: Tyndale, 1996.

———. *106 Questions Children Ask About Our World*. Wheaton, IL: Tyndale, 1998.

———. *107 Questions Children Ask About Prayer*. Wheaton, IL: Tyndale, 1998.

———. *108 Questions Children Ask About Friends and School*. Wheaton, IL: Tyndale, 1999.

———. *801 Questions Kids Ask About God*. Wheaton, IL: Tyndale, 2000.

Ideas for Prayer
- Thank God for making Himself known to us.
- Ask God to help you answer your children's questions about Him in a way that they can appreciate and understand.

Prayer for Kids
Here is a sample prayer your children can use.

"Dear Father, I have lots of questions about You. Thank You for letting me ask them, and please help me find and understand the answers. In Jesus' name, amen."

Answers to Prayer

MOM, I THINK I GOT A BUSY SIGNAL.

Answers to Prayer

Help us, O God, to receive the fulfillment of all our requests. Let us not doubt that you have heard and will hear them; that the answer is certain, not negative or doubtful. So may we say cheerfully that the outcome is true and certain. Amen.

Martin Luther

Young children are naturally trusting. It's easy for them to believe that God will answer their prayers. However, we need to encourage that trust. Such encouragement should come in the form of strengthening the picture they have of God and His ability and willingness to hear and answer.

Faith and Doubt

Before we discuss our children's possible doubts, let's look at our own. Sometimes our children may be more willing to trust than we are. If that happens, the natural thing that will come into your mind is, *What if it doesn't work? What if God doesn't answer? My children will be hurt and disappointed and won't want to pray and get to know God anymore!*

Time out. This fear—which we all go through—if acted on consistently, could end up causing your children not to expect anything from God. As a result, their prayer life could just become a ritual.

When the clouds of doubt start blocking out the sun, go into your prayer closet and tell God you're having trouble believing. Ask Him to help clear away your doubts, be still and let Him settle your heart, and look up Scriptures to confirm or dislodge what you have in your heart. We all worry from time to time; doubts parade through, tracking their muddy "fearprints" all over our brains. It's what we do with them that counts. We can believe them and let them set up camp in our thoughts, or we can go to God, tell Him how we feel, choose to believe, and ask Him to help us chase them off.

Faith isn't a magical substance that we build up in a spiritual vial until we have enough. It's a choice.

When one father asked Jesus to deliver his son from convulsions and an evil spirit, he asked in weak faith, "If you can do anything, take pity on us and help us." After Jesus said to the father, "Everything is possible for him who believes," the father declared, "I do believe; help me overcome my unbelief!" (Mark 9:22–24). He responded honestly to Jesus' request for faith, saying, in effect, "I believe and I choose to believe, but I have doubts. Can You help me with them?" Jesus responded by healing his boy.

Jesus said that if we have faith as small as a mustard seed, we could move mountains (see Matthew 17:20). Faith isn't a magical substance that we build up in a spiritual vial until we have enough. It's a choice. The father didn't ask for more faith. He chose to believe and then asked Jesus to help him with the doubts. He had a very small amount of faith, probably the size of a mustard seed, but he got great results.

Don't be ashamed of doubt; it's a normal part of the process. Just handle it with prayer. And look to "Jesus, the author and perfecter of our faith" (Hebrews 12:2). Remember, God invented the faith process so that we could be sure of His help. We make the choice to believe and call on His mercy to help the doubts clear away like clouds on a windy day.

Reflections

1. What kinds of situations test your faith in God? Why?

    _____

    _____

    _____

    _____

    What helps you get through these situations?

    _____

    _____

    _____

2. What kinds of situations test your children's faith in God?

    _____

    _____

    _____

    Are they the same for each child? Why or why not?

    _____

    _____

    _____

3. How can you help your children get through these situations?

    _____

    _____

    _____

"Conditions" to Answered Prayer

We've all heard there are conditions to answered prayer. But if God set prayer up to be dependent only on His mercy and grace not on our performance or goodness, how can there be conditions? Aren't grace and conditions contrary to each other?

Good question. The answer is yes, they are contrary. What we sometimes think of as conditions are really just parts of our growth process and relationship with God.

1. God's Will

God cannot violate His Word, which declares His will. And, of course, His will does not conflict with answers according to His grace and mercy. His will is determined by what is best for us, by love, and by His mercy—and they are not contrary to each other! God will not deny us what is best just because He decides not to. His will aligns with His character. Since He is love, His will always includes what is best for us. Therefore, His will is not a limiting condition but the expression of His love and His best.

2. Faith and Trust

These are not conditions demanding performance, but God's system for making it all depend on His unchanging character, rather than on our ever-changing performance. Grace, not law. Again, these are not limiting conditions but our guaranteed access to God's wonderful grace.

3. Our Growth and Performance in Christ

There is a perception that, as we become more mature Christians and gain experience at prayer, we will receive more answers. The thought is that maturity breeds "success" in prayer. This statement is both true and false.

The statement is false because, regardless of our children's maturity, God will always answer their prayers according to their faith in His grace—not according to their performance. Yet the statement is true because, as our children understand the truth of God's love and faithfulness, their prayer lives will grow and become more effective. After all, the core of being a Christian is developing a relationship with God and having Him be our heavenly Father, letting Him take care of us and help us grow to be all that He has created us to be. Based on that relationship—not our performance—we receive more answers.

Your child's growth and performance can be compared to that of a garden. Many combined factors affect growth. A plant must have oxygen, water, soil, nutrients, and sunshine to grow. Then it grows stems, leaves, flowers, and finally fruit. Humans are the most complex of God's creatures. When healthy conditions exist, every part of us grows in His order and in unison. I don't know how it works, but God created us to grow evenly in a way that keeps us balanced. For example, with the understanding of being forgiven comes the responsibility for and understanding of forgiving others.

When healthy conditions exist, every part of us grows in His order and in unison.

As we get to know God more intimately, we trust Him more and for more. Our understanding of who He wants us to be, how He wants us to act, and what He wants us to do grows as well. This changes what we trust Him for. That's the dynamic of growth.

Simply put, we grow in faith and in the results of our prayer life as we grow in our relationship with God and as we see corresponding growth in every area of our lives as Christians. But that is a process that God has set up for our blessing. It is not to be understood as "being a good Christian and doing good things will motivate God to answer you." Receiving from God is by faith in His grace alone. He loves your children and is faithful. Once again, the need for Christian growth is not a limiting condition. Instead, this element can help us to become intimate with His love and His grace.

4. Confessing Sin

When our children sin, we need to remind them of the wonderful Bible promise: "If we confess our sins, he is faithful and just and will forgive us our sins and purify us from all unrighteousness" (1 John 1:9).

The growth process we just talked about is progressive. If our children blow it, it's important that we let them know they have made a mistake and need to be forgiven. We should have them pray and ask God to forgive them—not because He's mad at them but because He wants the best for them, will help them do better, and will give them wisdom and strength. He's like the coach who says to the player who just repeated his mistake in the game, "It's OK, you're a good player. I'll help you with that so you'll do better next time." We should never send our children to ask God to forgive them when we are angry. God is not angry with them: He wants to help them grow.

Mistakes our children make as they learn and grow will not hinder their prayers being answered.

During the growth process, God recognizes that we aren't perfect. As a parent, don't require your child to ask for forgiveness for every little mistake or for all the sins he may have committed. This puts a wrong focus on the process and puts God in the position of a demanding judge, not a loving Father. The Holy Spirit is well able, as we all know, to give us that nudge when we've crossed the line and need to get things right with God. We should teach our kids this same process.

Yes, staying in sin, not confessing it to God, or continuing in it even though we know it's wrong, will block the prayer process, but there aren't many children in that camp. The mistakes our children make as they learn and grow will not hinder their prayers being answered.

5. Forgiving Others

Asking forgiveness brings up another perceived condition to answered prayer: forgiving others. But this is not a performance condition; on the contrary, it amplifies the point that we can only receive answers to prayer by God's mercy and grace.

God is merciful and forgiving to us even though we don't deserve it. (This is grace.) He requires that we demonstrate our understanding of that by forgiving anyone who may do or say something to us we don't like. We are to forgive them not because they deserve it but because we, like our heavenly Father, are to be merciful.

If your children (or you) are unable to automatically choose to forgive those whom they believe have wronged them, they probably don't understand fully the concepts of mercy and forgiveness. And if they don't understand those concepts, they are asking God to forgive them because they think that, as they are usually good enough, they deserve to be forgiven. No one ever deserves to be forgiven. Likewise, we should never require those who wrong us to deserve our absolute and instant forgiveness.

Of course, your child may resent the need to forgive others. "But they haven't asked me to forgive them, or even admitted they've done anything wrong! They say it's my fault!" Tell him it does not matter. Our friends (and enemies) don't have to deserve forgiveness. After all, we don't. Teach your child to automatically say, "God, I forgive them. Please help us to get along with each other and treat each other the way you want us to."

Jesus' words are clear: "For if you forgive men when they sin against you, your heavenly Father will also forgive you. But if you do not forgive men their sins, your Father will not forgive your sins" (Matthew 6:14–15).

Yet this seeming condition to prayer, like the others, does not contradict our receiving God's grace. It is a response to God's grace. Indeed, every part of our lives, including our prayers, centers around trusting in His grace.

Reflections

1. Based on what you read, what conditions do you think need to be met before God will answer your prayers?

2. Think of a time when your prayers weren't answered the way you wanted. What did you learn from this experience that you wouldn't have learned if God had done things just the way you asked?

3. How can you use this experience to teach your children about answers to prayer?

_____

_____

_____

Patiently Waiting for the Answer

"Are we there yet?"

Once your child has prayed, he realizes, for the most part, that the answer won't be there when he opens his eyes. The patience of young children seems to short-circuit when they know that what they are excited about is close. I'm sure it's more a total lack of a concept of passing time than it is a lack of patience.

Patience is the evidence of trust and the partner of faith. As the writer of Hebrews noted, "We do not want you to become lazy, but to imitate those who through faith and patience inherit what has been promised" (Hebrews 6:12).

Actually, few young children have a problem with praying about something and then just leaving it with God. But as they get older, they may need to understand three timing issues that will help them maintain their patience:

1. It Takes Time

Although God can do anything He wants when He wants, He seems to answer our prayers, more often than not, in the natural course of events. When your child prays for God's help to do better in school, the answer will probably involve better study habits, better concentration during class, a keener desire to learn, and other natural things. A prayer for a new bike may involve a lesson in saving and an opportunity to earn extra money. Even if the bicycle shows up with a gift bow on it, the process from prayer to bicycle had to move through people, a few decisions, and someone's bank account. And the actual delivery might not get there until your child's birthday months later.

One morning at breakfast, promise your child her favorite

dessert. If she asks you about it during the day, tell her to be patient. Say, "I promised, so you'll get it." Don't say when. Wait until the latest possible time, then go out and get the ingredients. Make it and put it aside while you do something else. At the last possible moment, perhaps when she is about to climb into bed, call her to the table and serve it.

While eating dessert, draw the parallel to prayer. When we ask God about or for something, He hears and answers. It may take time to get there, but just like the dessert, once you told your child she was going to have it, it was as good as hers. Only the timing was in question. This exercise is easy and your child will remember it whenever she's trying to wait patiently for her prayers to be answered.

> **Patience is the evidence of trust and the partner of faith.**

2. God's Timing Is Perfect

Here's an explanation that your child will love: "God loves everyone, knows everything, can do anything, and is everywhere all at once. Now, when He answers one person's prayer, He knows and considers all the effects that answering that prayer will have on everything and everyone, everywhere—now and in the future. Compound that by billions of prayer requests daily. God has no problem making all of those calculations and decisions in an instant, or in figuring out how He will answer every prayer and how that will affect everyone else. He is limitless."

That awesome picture of God will excite and probably boggle your child's mind. Then remind him of this simple truth: God usually works through people and natural events. Finally, assure him of God's wise plan: "God's calculation has considered the perfect answer at the perfect time for you, and that's when it will get here. It may not be when you expected it, but it will be perfect."

3. Never Give Up

Winston Churchill was asked to speak to the graduating class of a university. Everyone was set to hear a profound, stirring address. He walked out onto the platform and said, "Never, never, never give up!" and walked off again.

Our children (and we) should never give up on their prayers. God never forgets or loses track of any of them. I've had times when I completely forgot I had prayed about a certain thing and, years later, the prayer was answered. Then I remembered. At times, money came through at the perfect time for me to use it for the exact purpose for which I had asked God in the first place.

I've seen God answer prayers of mine ten years later. At the time I prayed, I thought I needed it then. But years later, when the answer came and I remembered the prayer, I looked back on the time I prayed and realized that I was not ready for the answer then. God considers the timing and responsibility factors for our own good. If your children wanted to learn to drive a car when they were twelve, the answer wouldn't be no, the answer would be, "You're not ready for that yet. We'll do it when you're older."

Prayers are often like seeds: You plant them now and they pop up sometime in the future.

Teach your children to pray in a way that leaves everything in God's hands. Then let them know that God considers everything and, all factors considered, starts to move the answer toward us and us toward the answer. Let them know that prayers are often like seeds: You plant them now and they pop up sometime in the future. Encourage your children to never get so wrapped up in receiving answers, that they feel like giving up or deciding that God isn't answering. Help them get excited about getting closer to God, trusting their whole lives more and more into His hands, and leaving every single prayer completely in His care. He'll always do what is best when it's the best time for Him to do it. Remember, the purpose of prayer is to have a relationship with our heavenly Father, not to place an order.

Reflections

What are some things your children are praying for right now?

_____

_____

Talk to them about it, and help them to test whether what they are praying for lines up with God's will, as expressed in the Bible. How can they change their prayers so they line up better with God's will?

Testing of Our Faith

The Bible tells us clearly that God is faithful, that He hears and answers our prayers, and helps us to grow. But nowhere in the Bible does God tell us that life will be without its bumps and bruises. Even when we have a great relationship with God and an awesome prayer life, we still live in a fallen world that tends to dump a little garbage into everyone's lives. We must prepare our children for the testing of their faith. God says it will happen. And James explains that God is often the author of it (but not of evil, as we will discuss in the next section):

> Consider it pure joy, my brothers, whenever you face trials of many kinds, because you know that the testing of your faith develops perseverance. Perseverance must finish its work so that you may be mature and complete, not lacking anything. (James 1:2–4)

Some of the most awesome, faith-inspiring faith stories I have to tell my children have been at the end of difficult trials. Some of the biggest life lessons I've learned, resulting in God developing me as a person, were also attached to these events. Our trials make us grow as individuals, or, as James wrote, "mature and complete, not lacking anything" (verse 4).

A good way to explain this truth to your child is have her picture a very scary, tall roller coaster. "You're about to board, and you have second thoughts about getting on. When you finally step on and sit down, your heart is pumping and you feel you may soon scream. But the thing that makes it OK is that you know it's safe and you'll be back on solid ground in a little while." Explain that when God is using life's experiences to test our faith, it's like that roller coaster; eventually we will return in safety.

Does that mean you shouldn't pray and talk to God along the way, just because you know it will work out okay? No, this is a time to run to God. You need His wisdom, guidance, strength, and help clearing away the doubt clouds. The whole reason for our faith being tested is for us to learn, get stronger, and get closer to God. (You may want to point your child to 1 Peter 1:7.) Besides, not praying while you're going through a trial is like falling asleep on a roller coaster—almost impossible!"

If your child doesn't understand this principle, he may get discouraged and think God doesn't care or isn't willing to answer and help. Help him understand and hang on. The greatest faith story he has is probably just beyond the next roller-coaster loop.

When Our Children Can't Understand the Tough Times

The apostle Paul traveled through much of the Roman Empire. A few times he was unable to preach the gospel. Once Paul wanted to go somewhere and Satan stopped him (1 Thessalonians 2:18); another time the Holy Spirit kept him from going (Acts 16:6); and in other places natural causes, such as bad weather, prevented him from getting places.

Paul knew to ultimately trust that everything was in God's hands and that God would work it all together for good. "And we know that in all things God works for the good of those who love him, who have been called according to his purpose" (Romans 8:28).

Your child need not understand all the whys. Although God is sovereign, and ultimately works everything out in accordance with His own purposes, there is ample evidence in the Bible that He is not the direct cause of every event or problem that happens in our lives. (When we stub our little toe, do we say God did that?)

When teaching our children, therefore, we should not automatically blame God for things that are inconsistent with His love and character. I'm not saying to oversimplify and tell them everything they like is from God and everything they don't is from the devil. A lot of things like spinach and broccoli would be on the wrong list. I'm just saying if you're not sure (and you're not), don't use God as a catchall scapegoat for everything that is difficult to explain.

If you wouldn't kill your child's cat to teach her something, neither would God.

If your child's cat gets hit by a car, it's better to tell her you don't understand why things happen and pray with her for God to comfort her (and possibly help you find a new cat). Don't say, "God must have needed Tiger in heaven," or "God always does things for a reason. Maybe we needed to learn something." Chances are, if you wouldn't kill your child's cat to teach her something, neither would God. When you don't understand, don't blame God; direct your child to Him for help and wisdom. He's not the problem; He's the solution.

We need to teach our children from a very young age that it's not necessary to understand everything. The following picture can help your child understand God's motives even when he doesn't fully understand God's ways. (It's a simple allegory, not a theological presentation.)

Your child is the mountain climber, and life is climbing a mountain. God, the master mountaineer, is climbing with your child. He teaches him how to climb and helps your child on the way to the top. "The purpose of the climb isn't just to get you to the top or He could just carry you there. The purpose is to make you into a great climber and a better person. God won't cause you to fall and break your neck. He won't cause a rock to fall on your head. And He won't leave you stranded on the mountain lost and dying.

"Might a rock fall on your head? Yes! Did God do it to teach you something? No! Will He help you recover and get back on the mountain? Yes!

"Now when you come to a difficult part of the climb and think you can't do it, will He just lift you up and put you at the next level? No! (Say math looks too tough and you'd rather play soccer; will God learn it for you or let you ignore it? No! Prayer is not a shortcut!) Will He give you wisdom, encouragement, and strength to help you figure it out and take the next step? Yes! If it's absolutely impossible to climb, will He miraculously help you up? Yes! Will He purposely lead you to a more difficult route up the mountain, to teach and strengthen you and prepare you for even greater climbing feats? Yes! Will He give you peace, joy, encouragement, and praise, and help to clear away the fears on the way up? Yes! Will He provide the gear, food, and fellowship you need on the way up? Yes!"

We need to teach our children that it's not necessary to understand everything.

Explain that there are many routes to the summit, yet God has one particular route mapped out that will challenge the child to use all his gifts and help him to serve his fellow climbers in a way that's perfect for him. "If you follow that route, has God already made sure there aren't large loose rocks that will fall on your head? Most likely! He's trustworthy."

Remind your child of the Bible's declaration that we can rejoice during sufferings because they bring perseverance, character, and a hope that does not disappoint (Romans 5:3–5).

Tips and Suggestions

Many times God answers our children's prayers by giving them the opportunity, ability, or wisdom to solve the problem themselves. For example, if they pray for a material thing, God may give them the opportunity to earn some extra money and buy it themselves. Prayer for restoration in a friendship may require your son or daughter to seek the person out to discuss their problem.

When your child is asking for something specific from God, help her add feet to her prayers. First, she can ask God for help to know if there is anything she can do. Have her be quiet for a moment and think about it before plowing into more prayers. Discuss possible options. The key to answered prayer can come through a suggestion from someone else. Then have your child commit to God any efforts she may undertake. Expect God to work things out for your child as she goes forward.

One of the most important things you can mentor concerning answered prayer is faithfulness. A family motto we use is "If I say, I'll do. If I say it's the truth, you can count on it." It almost becomes a game because our children know that if they can get us to say we'll do something, take them somewhere, or give them something, the rest is academic; it's as good as theirs. When your children see that you are always faithful to your word, it's easy for them to understand how they can count on God.

Be careful when deciding to help answer your children's prayers. Many times you will be the source and channel of delivery for an answer to prayer, yet don't automatically assume it. God doesn't have to have your help. Pray about it yourself and wait a bit. Make sure everything seems right about you doing it or buying it for them.

When you think you're to be the answer, tell your children you prayed about it and many times God uses parents to answer kids' prayers. Providing for children is part of the parents' job. If, however, it just doesn't seem right, wait. God may have another solution that will help your children see His love and hand at work in their lives in a different way.

These activities will help increase your children's confidence in God and His power to answer prayer.

Activity: Answer Trackers and Treasure Hunters

1. Turn your children into *"answer trackers."* Children often will pray about something and then forget it. Even when they don't forget, they may not make the connection between their prayers and the answers. That's where you come in, especially with younger children. Remember the things that your children have prayed about and when the answers come, point them out. Track those answers to prayer. Point out that the answer gives them another faith story to record and talk about. You might even want to have your kids start their own Faith Story book with that first answer. Buy them nice blank books (or use the ones you made earlier) and have them write the answers down. Help them remember to go back to God and thank Him.

2. Let your children play the "Find the Treasure" game. Hide candy around the house. Have your spouse join in the fun (or another adult, if you're a single parent). The second adult should not know where the candy is. Now tell the kids about the candy. Let them know they can ask the two adults any questions that require a "yes" or "no" answer to try and find the candy. Once the game has begun, the second adult should say vague things like, "Well, I really can't tell you that," or "I don't think I can answer that." After a while it will become clear that the only one with the ability to reveal the whereabouts of the candy is you.

3. Once the candy is found and your children are enjoying it, draw the parallel: There seems to be more than one way to get what we want in life. But God is the only One who really knows what is best and has the ability to give it to us every time. Ask your kids, "So why waste time pursuing things? Pursue God and He becomes your source for everything."

Questions

1. What do we mean when we say that God is "testing" our faith?

_____

_____

_____

Why does He do this?

_____

_____

_____

2. Describe a recent experience when you felt your faith was being tested by God. What were the circumstances? What did you learn from the experience? How might you use this experience to teach your children about faith?

_____

_____

_____

_____

_____

_____

Ideas for Prayer
- Thank God for showing you that He is bigger than any situation you will ever face.
- Thank God for promising to supply you with everything you need when the going gets tough.
- Ask God to increase your faith in Him, and to show you what you can do to help build up your children's faith in Him as well.

Prayer for Kids
Here is a sample prayer your children can use.

"Dear Father, thank You for helping me each day. Please help me to trust that You know the best way to answer all of my prayers. In Jesus' name, amen."

Teaching Some of the How-to Details

Teaching Some of the How-to Details

A prayer is not holy chewing gum and you don't have to see how far you can stretch it.

Lionel Blue

As parents, we are more than guardians who raise and protect our children until they become adults. We are teachers and mentors, not just of concepts and principles but also of the practical how-to mechanics of life. This includes the mechanics of prayer. Let's consider several areas.

How to Open and Close in Prayer

In teaching His disciples about life after His death and resurrection, Jesus told them to pray to the Father in His name (see John 15:16; 16:23–24, 26–27). This is also the way Paul prayed (see Ephesians 1:17; Colossians 1:3). Although the greater volume of Scripture says to pray to the Father, some speak of praying to Jesus.

Jesus is God. He's not God the Father, but He is one Person of the Trinity. So when our children pray to Jesus, they are going to the same authority. But for the sake of teaching them what prayer is and how to do it, it's good to direct them to open and close in prayer consistent with the biblical pattern. This involves three basic elements: (1) the address: "Our Father"; (2) the authority, or "who says": "In Jesus' name"; and (3) the close: "amen." These elements hold the potential for some very basic lessons that will serve as positive reminders every time they pray.

1. The Address

Every time our children address their prayer to God their Father, they are reminded of the father allegory. God wants us to address Him as Father so that, coming into each prayer, we are reminded of the fact that He made us, loves us, and wants to take care of us. The address frames your children's prayers. Their prayers are heard by the loving and caring heavenly Father who wants to build a relationship with them and to help guide, teach, and give them wisdom.

God wants us to address Him as Father so that we are reminded that He made us, loves us, and wants to take care of us.

Teach your child to start every prayer by addressing her heavenly Father and what that means. When your child hears the word "dentist," she knows where she is going, what that person is going to do, and why. When she says "Father" at the beginning of her prayer, the same should be true. Have your child expand the address, or expand it for her from time to time to give her the idea: "Dear loving and awesome Father in heaven who takes care of me, . . ."

Also, do we need to address God every time we pray? Can't we just be walking down the road and start talking to Him? He's always there listening and knows I'm talking to Him, right? Yes, He is, and of course you can. But just as we teach our children rules for conversation, for the sake of clear communication and showing respect for others, we should teach them to address God each time they want to talk to Him. This calls their attention to who God is, demonstrates respect for Him, and helps your child know there is a line that separates what he is thinking from what he decides to talk to God about.

2. The Authority, or "Who Says"

The authority is in the name of Jesus, so we do not have to say, "in Jesus' name" every time we pray in order to be heard. God doesn't cull out the prayers without three words attached. When we become God's children, the line of communication is opened between us and our heavenly Father because of Jesus' death for us and our acceptance of it, because of Jesus or "in Jesus' name." In other words, we don't need permission to talk to the Father. We already have the authority to do that, thanks to Jesus' once and for all payment for our sins.

Yet I believe our children should say, "in Jesus' name" when they pray. When we teach them what the phrase means, "in Jesus' name" can become a wonderful reminder of three things:

1. *God's grace.* We can pray and be assured of God's love and care, not because we deserve it but because Jesus died for us. Saying "in Jesus' name" reminds us of that gracious act.

2. *God's listening and answering.* Nothing can stand in the way of our prayers being heard and answered by God. Nothing! Jesus' name, the Scripture declares, is "above [more important and more powerful than] every name" (Philippians 2:9).

3. *God's will.* The third reminder is a filter. We cannot pray something in Jesus' name that is not in line with Jesus'—and therefore God's—will. God takes all that we pray, filters it through His perfect will for us, and works out everything accordingly.

Once we've taught our children these three things, the words "in Jesus' name" will remind them of these truths. In effect, it's a reminder that, "Because of Jesus, I know You love me and hear and answer my prayers. I know that nothing is impossible for You and nothing can prevent You from hearing and answering me. And I know that You see the big picture and will answer me according to Your will, which is always best for me."

3. The Close

Last, is the close, "amen." The word means "may it become" or "so let it be!" "It is equated with the certainty of the promises of God!"[1] Do we need to say "amen" at the end of every prayer in order for it to be sent, like hitting the send button after typing an

E-mail message? No. But again the word "amen" as part of our prayers can serve a great purpose.

First, it can help in concentration. "Amen" helps us separate our time in conversation with God from our own time thinking or from conversation with others. Until the word "amen" is uttered, our children know that their concentration is to be on their relationship and communication with God.

Second, and more importantly, saying the word "amen" is saying we trust God and know that He has already heard and answered our prayers. When you're teaching your children why we say "amen," have them end their prayers (or you do it) with an expanded version, "Thank You, God, for hearing and answering my prayers. I know that these things I've talked to You about are all being taken care of according to Your Word and will!" In short, "amen" is a constant reminder to end our prayers in faith, knowing God has heard and answered.

Balance Between Business and Pleasure Prayers

In any ongoing relationship, there are two types of communication:

1. "Business communication" occurs when we discuss the business and necessary details that surround our relationship. For example, in a parent/child relationship, we must discuss things like the performance (or lack thereof) of certain chores, their schoolwork, their financial needs, and so on.

2. "Pleasure communication" can be about anything: how we feel, what we like, what we thought of something. This kind of communication helps us get to know each other better and allows us to enjoy each other and share some of ourselves.

Prayer is no different. The Bible outlines things that we and our children should talk to God about on a regular basis: business communication. But God doesn't want our children to stop there. He wants them to develop pleasure communication as well, telling Him how they feel, what their desires are, what they've been thinking about, and asking Him about what He's thinking and wants for their lives.

It is important for us to teach our children that, as in conversation with people, some parts of conversation with God tend to be more structured and others more freewheeling. Structured business communication with God might involve praying a heartfelt but memorized prayer or Bible verses.

The Bible calls us to pray for those in authority over us, so we should encourage our children to pray for us, their teachers, the police, our government, and so on. When our children pray for their teachers, the prayer might be very similar to what they prayed last time. That's OK. It's kind of like, "Can I go out?" "Have you done your homework yet?" "No, I was thinking of doing it later." "Please do your homework before you go out." That exact piece of business communication, or a very similar one, may happen many times. However, that should not be all prayer is. As your children get older, they'll be able to understand, from being involved in more conversations, the idea of freewheeling communication: talking from the heart about anything and everything.

Some parts of conversation with God tend to be more structured and others more freewheeling.

Use this same people/relationship conversation parallel to explain the need for both business and pleasure communication with God. A good way to teach this is to cover some business conversation with your children; then start up some pleasure conversation. When you are finished, point out the differences and draw the parallel.

Reflections

1. Do your prayers tip more toward business or pleasure?

_____

_____

_____

Keep a prayer diary over the next week and keep track of how many of your prayers are about business and how many are about pleasure. How did things turn out?

_____

_____

_____

Make a list of five things you can do to help bring your prayer life into more of a balance.

_____

_____

_____

_____

_____

2. When you pray with your children, do you or they tend to focus more on business or pleasure?

_____

_____

_____

What are some things you can do to help restore balance in your children's prayer lives?

_____

_____

_____

Memorized and Liturgical Prayers

The purpose behind prayer is never lengthy time in prayer nor the beauty of the content and words; it's developing a relationship with the heavenly Father and learning to rely on and receive from Him. Memorized prayers can be a beautiful, inspirational, and even practical way to help our children learn to pray. But there are some cautions. Once something is memorized, the temptation is to allow our mouths to say it while our heads and hearts are on another planet. Talk with your children about the meaning of the prayer before and while they are memorizing it. Make sure they understand. Encourage them to slow down and think about the prayer and what they are saying to God while they are praying it. You might have them make a freewheeling comment after the prayer, like "I really mean that, Father!"

Memorized prayers can be a beautiful, inspirational, and even practical way to help our children learn to pray.

Memorized prayer should be only a small addition to your children's prayer lives. After praying any sort of rote prayer, your children should be encouraged to pray other prayers. Most children do not possess the level of concentration needed to think through, mean, and apply their faith to a series of memorized prayers. Leading them through only memorized prayers will not help them achieve a heartfelt love relationship with God.

Overcoming Repetition, Overcoming Repetition

Every child will tend to find a certain set of prayers he knows both you and he like and press the replay button night after night. The child thinks, *If it's right, why fix it?*

The first two things to remember are, don't let it drive you crazy and don't let your child stay there. The second two are, don't let it drive you crazy and don't let your child stay there. (I couldn't resist.)

Start when your child is young by helping him add one different prayer each night, one that is unique to his day. Talk to him about the day, his concerns or upcoming events, and find something he would like to pray about. Tell him how God could help and how he can pray about the issue. As your child grows a little older, expand the prayer list by teaching him different types of prayers and things to talk to God about until each night his current prayer list takes up more time than the things he likes to repeat. You'll find that somewhere in this process your child will get the idea that prayer is a current affairs event, and his repetition prayers will drop down to two or three favorites.

How About Our Position in Prayer?

To kneel or not to kneel—that is the question. The Bible is full of examples of people praying in all manner of positions. It does not prescribe one: the position seems to be dictated by the type of prayer and the attitude of the petitioner. Sometimes, when someone like Moses expected God to be angry and he needed His mercy, he was on the ground on his face. When David was celebrating God's goodness and praising Him, he danced. Elijah and others, when praying in public, stood up. This was probably so everyone else involved in the prayer could hear. Another time, when Elijah was praying earnestly that it would rain, he prayed on the ground with his head between his knees. Earnest prayer calls for great concentration, and this position probably helped him concentrate. There is no right and wrong way.

The position seems to be dictated by the type of prayer and the attitude of the petitioner.

For the sake of teaching our children about position, consider these three elements: respect, concentration, and body language. Again, using a people/conversation parallel, our children understand we expect them to demonstrate respect for us when we speak by being still and looking at us. In terms of concentration, we remind them that they rarely focus on our words if they're fidgeting with a toy or have one ear still tuned to the television. In terms of body language, when we are correcting our children, they know that they should not be standing with their backs turned and their hands on their hips. Clearly, our children show others how they feel by how they position their bodies. Once your children understand this, help them demonstrate respect by staying still; help them understand that praying with their eyes closed will help them concentrate; and tell them they can change their position depending on how they feel.

If prayer time is at bedtime, then your child is probably lying down. If she tends to fall asleep quickly, this may not be a good idea. Have her sit on the edge of the bed or kneel by the bed. Here are a few other tips to help concentration.

- If your child has a bedtime snack or drink, provide it immediately after prayer is finished. Knowing the snack is coming will help her concentrate and get down to business.
- If your child is a squirmer and wants to play around, let him know you'll play with him for a few minutes and then he needs to stay still and pray. If he starts to squirm during prayer, just wait until he's done; then start up again.
- Remove all toys, teddy bears, and distractions. If a complaint is registered, let her know how important it is to be still and concentrate when she's talking to someone and promise to return the desired object as soon as prayer time is done.
- Keep the child interested! If concentration is at a particularly low ebb, make it short and quick before your child starts to fidget. Pray about something he is excited about. Then praise him for staying still (for those thirty seconds). Build on that the next night.
- Change the position from time to time depending on what is going on. If you go on prayer walks, take her for one. If you like to sit at a desk with pen and paper handy when you pray, let your child try that. If there is a particularly serious thing to pray about, suggest that you get down on your knees together. (Don't use the knees position if you are teaching about asking God for forgiveness. This can be remembered as embarrassing or demeaning. For children, God's love for them and His desire to help them get it right for their sake should be emphasized. A quick "Sorry, God, help me do better," accompanied by praise and hugs is what is needed.)

Praying Out Loud or Silently

There are examples of both silent and spoken personal prayers in the Bible. Obviously, if the prayer is a group or public prayer, it needs to be out loud. When you are praying with your child and teaching him to pray, audible prayers are the only kind you can use: You can't help if you can't hear the prayer. But there may be times when your child may not want to pray a certain prayer out loud. In this case, encourage him to pray it silently and let you know when he is done.

When your child is older and starts to say her prayers primarily on her own, she may want to say them silently. If she is having trouble concentrating, though, encourage her to speak the prayer aloud, even if it's hardly audible.

How Long Should Your Child Pray?

It's not how long your child prays that counts. Jesus told us not to babble on and think that God hears us just because we talk a lot. Learning a bunch of prayer formulas or memorized prayers that are repeated to fill up the desired time is babbling on. Similarly, if we try to make time the primary goal, the time spent becomes relatively meaningless.

Instead, as we gradually teach our children the things the Bible tells us to pray about and help them develop a desire to know God better, the time they want and need to spend in prayer will automatically increase. The more a person gets to know God and learn about prayer, the longer he spends in prayer.

Spending a half hour to one hour in daily prayer is a good life goal. They need to know the goal they are ultimately aiming for; yet the key to getting them there is to teach them more about prayer and get them excited about it. Let that process take as long as it takes.

Mealtime Prayers and Learning to Pray with Others

The best place for a child to first experience praying in front of others is at home. The first step is to see and hear you pray with the family. A comfortable next step is having your child pray with you at a time other than prayer time. When your son (or daughter) is comfortable praying and would like the privilege, let him say the mealtime prayer. This is an awesome venue for teaching and training your child to pray with others. Mealtime prayers should be kept simple when your child is young so that he can understand and learn to pray by taking part.

When your child first says the prayer, let it be short and quick, maybe even repeated after you. Praise him instantly for his effort, encouraging him. Don't force your child to pray in a group. Ask him if he would like to pray. If he declines, that's OK. Talk to him about it afterward, when you're alone, to find out why he declined and encourage him forward. It's not a good idea to ask a child who is just getting started in group prayer to pray for a meal when you have guests. (Unless of course he or she is the superoutgoing type who wants to do so.)

The best place for a child to first experience praying in front of others is at home.

When the child is at the point where you think it would be good for her to take a next step and pray with guests present, ask her ahead of time to avoid embarrassing her. When one of your children is saying the mealtime prayer, encourage her to say it a little differently each time or add a current family request.

When praying out loud in front of people, it's easy to get so distracted by what you are saying and how you are saying it, that you lose your focus. Help your children with this by teaching them to, first, quietly and privately ask God to help them pray and, second, encourage them that mealtime prayer is not just a ritual. They should believe that God has heard and answered their prayer.

This is a good time to teach the difference between group and personal prayers. Simply put, group prayers are about and for the concerns of the group. Personal prayers address your concerns, for yourself or others. Mealtime prayers are not a time to pray about all the family's concerns. They should be brief, thanking God for the food, asking Him to bless it, and maybe covering one other hot topic. Then eat. If you spend a lot of time praying when everyone is hungry, they won't be concentrating or learning; they'll just want to eat. In group prayer, although one person prays out loud, all others should be concentrating as if the words were their own, focusing on God and agreeing with what is being said.

If you want to have a family prayer time, when you all pray together for the family's needs, call it when everyone will be excited about the event. You might call a special family prayer time only when a particular issue comes up that warrants it. Before bed at everyone's prayer time is perfect. First, the children are expecting to pray then, and second, it will be a creative change to the usual routine. If you want a regular family prayer time, you could plan it once a week at the usual bedtime prayer time. Or keep it distinctly separate, choosing a time that doesn't cause disgruntled or distracted participants. Plan it ahead of time and let everyone know (excitedly) when it's going to be.

Keep the family prayer time short. Don't go beyond your children's ability to concentrate. Make it exciting. Maybe Family Prayer Night is also ice cream sundae night, so when prayers are over ice cream is served. Make sure prayer stays a positive experience. The easiest student to teach is one who is eager to learn and excited about applying the knowledge.

We need to purposely teach our children to pray in a group. If they are growing up in a Christian setting, they probably will be called on, or see the necessity themselves, to lead in prayer. Help them be prepared.

Questions

1. How were you first taught to pray?

_____

_____

_____

Was this method effective for you? Why or why not?

_____

_____

_____

2. How has your prayer life changed since you first became a Christian? Has it become more formal or less formal? More structured or less? Why?

_____

_____

_____

_____

_____

Ideas for Prayer

- Thank God for the pleasure it is to spend time with Him each day.
- Ask God to help you release your life to Him more fully, and to make prayer more about discovering His will than asking Him to affirm your will.
- Ask God to help you show your children how to balance the elements of "business" and "pleasure" in their prayer lives.

Prayer for Kids

Here is a sample prayer your children can use.

"Dear Father God, thank You that I can spend time with You each day. Please show me the right words to say when I pray. In Jesus' name, amen."

---

1. J. D. Douglas and Merrill C. Tenney, eds. *New International Dictionary of the Bible*, rev. ed. (Grand Rapids, Mich: Zondervan, 1988), s.v. "amen."

Teaching Your Child What to Pray

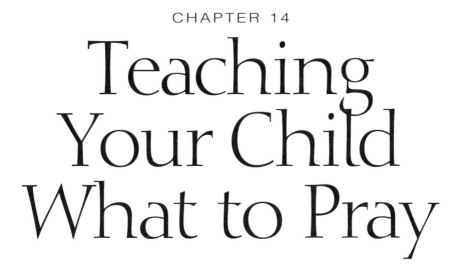

GOD, I'M REALLY TIRED. PLEASE JUST BLESS ME AND
EVERYONE ELSE, AMEN.

Teaching Your Child What to Pray

More things are wrought by prayer than this world dreams of.
Lord Tennyson

Our children need to know that they can talk to God about anything, anywhere, at anytime. But there are some things God specifically wants us to remember to talk to Him about, for example, people in authority over us. "I urge, then, first of all, that requests, prayers, intercession and thanksgiving be made for everyone—for kings and all those in authority, that we may live peaceful and quiet lives in all godliness and holiness" (1 Timothy 2:1–2).

In explaining that there are different things we should pray about, we should stay away from describing types of prayer using long, difficult titles. When we give prayer its own language and separate it into types and categories, we complicate it and unintentionally communicate that prayer is like learning a different language. And we are back to teaching our children to perform prayer.

We can explain prayer topics simply by comparing our children's conversation with us to their conversation with God. We pray about different things just as we talk to one another about all kinds of topics and issues. Our children ask us for what they need and desire. We have conversations about things that interest each of us, dates and events coming up, the needs and concerns of others and how we might help, the needs of the church, and how we can reach others for Christ. We talk to our children about their learning and growth process, discuss our relationship, ask each other for forgiveness, talk about elections and teachers, and thank one another.

> **We can explain prayer topics by comparing our children's conversation with us to their conversation with God.**

We do all this and call it conversation, not different types of talking. All these are things your child can talk to God about, too.

The Lord's Prayer: A Pattern for Praying

The Lord's Prayer (Matthew 6:9–13) is a good guide to all the basic things we need to pray about. Jesus gave it to His disciples as an outline to prayer and a lesson on our attitudes in prayer. Here is a simple summary of the meaning of each phrase using the New King James Version.

"Our Father in heaven." With these words Jesus introduced the New Testament idea of having a relationship with the heavenly Father. We can talk to Him and get to know Him.

"Hallowed be Your name." We are to give God honor for who He is and what He has done. Simply put for children, we are to thank Him.

"Your kingdom come." This is not just a prayer for the second coming of Jesus but for the growth and stability of the church. We need to pray for the spread of the gospel and for the strengthening of the church and of all Christians.

"Your will be done on earth as it is in heaven." Again, this is not just a prayer for the next age but one for submission to God's will in our lives and in the world around us. We need to pray for our leaders, those in authority around the world, and current affairs (see 1 Timothy 2:1–2).

"Give us this day our daily bread." Here we ask God to take care of us and meet our needs. We need to commit everything in our lives—all of our personal needs, desires, and concerns—to God.

"And forgive us our debts." The word debts does not refer to major sins but to us "falling short." We need to talk to God about our growth by His Spirit.

"As we forgive our debtors." We pray for others, not just those who do wrong to us but for all around us who fall short just like we do.

"And do not lead us into temptation, but deliver us from the evil one." We pray for God to lead us and keep us, for wisdom, guidance, and direction. We need to pray that we go God's way, not the way of the Evil One.

"For Yours is the kingdom and the power and the glory forever. Amen." God has the authority and power to fulfill His will and answer our prayers. He gets the credit for accomplishing His will in our lives and in the world around us. And we say "Amen," agreeing that God hears and answers our prayers.

Thank-You and Special-to-Me Prayers

How can you teach all of this information to your child? To start with, when she is very young, give her a bit at a time, as much as she can handle and understand. Start by teaching her to open and close. Then have her sandwich thank-you prayers (the child's version of "Hallowed be Your name"), and special-to-me prayers (the child's version of "Give us this day our daily bread" or praying for their needs and concerns) in between the "Dear Father" and "Amen." Thank-you prayers can include some general (and often repeated) thank-yous, and one or two specific to current, exciting events in her life. Special-to-me prayers can cover one or two current concerns, desires, and upcoming events relevant to your child.

Thus, a beginner's prayer may sound something like this. "Dear Father. I love You. Thank You for the ice cream we had today. Thank You for taking care of me. Please help me have a good birthday. Could You help me learn to ride my bike?

Thank You for answering my prayers and loving me. In Jesus' name, amen."

Other Prayers Derived from the Lord's Prayer

The other prayers can be added as they are needed. In other words, if you explain to your child the need to ask God for forgiveness and trust Him to help him learn, that evening would be a good time to introduce growing prayers. Such prayers are the children's version of "forgive us our debts," or praying for God to help us overcome our shortfalls and become more like He wants us to be. Once added, growing prayers can be expanded to, "Help me to be kind to my brother. Help me do things Your way because I know that's best." Always remember to keep it relevant. If telling the truth is a current issue, then "Remind me to always tell the truth" is a good growing prayer for that night.

Here are the other prayers that can be added as your child grows:

- Church prayers (the children's version of "Your kingdom come"). This includes prayers for God's will to be done in many areas. It might include prayers for a missionary your child met or heard about; prayer for a relative or friend who hasn't become a Christian yet; prayer for your church to be able to help more people.

- Leader prayers (children's version of "Your will be done on earth as it is in heaven"). Prayers for people in authority over your child, to start with: parents, teachers, politicians, Sunday school teachers, baby-sitters. As he or she gets older and understands, add prayer for world leaders and current events.

- Prayers for others (children's version of "as we also have forgiven our debtors"). Prayers for brothers and sisters, relatives, friends, people the child meets, and family friends.

- God's way prayers (children's version of "lead us not into temptation, but deliver us from the evil one"). Prayers for God's wisdom and direction in general or specific to an issue your child is facing. Prayers that God would help your child know and follow His plan for his life. Prayers that he would know and follow God's Word.

Some of these prayers help your child learn from a young age how God wants her to rely on Him and follow Him. If your child's prayers are only requests, she can grow up thinking that prayer is like the shopping channel. As parents we should continually remind our children that they need also to trust God, give Him their lives, and follow Him. We tell them that they can do their part in the body of Christ and in His army to help reach the lost. Teaching your child to pray about all of these things helps her grow up with a balanced life and a right view of who God is, who she is, and why she is here.

Keep the focus on communicating heartfelt issues with a real, listening God.

Remember, though, don't push this formula too hard. Use it as a help and guide, but make sure the prayers stay real and relevant. Once the formula or system is understood, work at dropping it, so that the focus stays on communicating heartfelt issues with a real, listening God. When you introduce a new topic to talk to God about, or even after you've taught all of them, it's not necessary to cover each one every day. The best times of prayer can be when you spend the entire time on one issue.

Your child will most often have prayers in some of the topics but not all. That's OK. It's better that his prayers are short and meaningful than that they are long and shallow. Help him come up with ideas while you're talking through the list. But let him decide which ones to pray about. Don't belabor the list or he'll get bored and lose interest. Encourage him forward and praise him as he takes on more.

A Poem About Children's Prayer

The following poem, entitled "The Things I Pray For," takes the different "children's version topics" from the Lord's Prayer and presents them in the same order but in an easy-to-understand way. It can help your children remember what to pray about. You can say it to them, and eventually with them, each night before going over your list. Make it fun. (Not all children will be helped by this. As we covered earlier, each child's relationship with God will grow differently.)

The Things I Pray For
God and I
and thank-yous many.
I pray for the church
and leaders plenty;
things special to me
and help to grow,
then I pray for others
and His way to go.
He hears my prayers
and answers them.
And in Jesus' name
I say "Amen."

Some children may want to memorize this poem and use it as a structure for composing their own prayers. Encourage them to have new and relevant prayer requests in the different categories each night. Also, encourage them to "freewheel" it a bit with pleasure communication under special-to-me prayers.

For Older Children

Here's an example of a prayer that an older child might say one night after he or she went through the poem. It also reflects the formula found in the Lord's Prayer and the above poem.

"Dear Father, I love You. I want to know You even more. You are always so good to me.

"Thank You for my family and for the camping trip we are going on. Please keep us safe and let us have lots of fun." (That is an example of not forcing the formula: Once your child brought up the camping trip as a thank-you prayer, it's best for him to talk to God about it until he is done.)

"Thank You for our church. Help the youth group have a good presentation on Friday. And could You show me how to make money for the missionary offering next month? Father, please give my teacher extra wisdom so she knows what to do when trouble happens again in the class. And give my parents wisdom for voting in the election.

"Father, my in-line skates are broken. Can You help me find a place to get them fixed or maybe I could get new ones? Either way I'd like to skate with Tammy again. And could You help me do my best for the test tomorrow? I like to do well in school.

"Thank You for helping me learn and grow. I know I need to be kind to my brother. Please remind me and help me. Also help me to understand more while I'm reading my Bible.

"Father, Tammy's dad needs a new job. Please help him find one. And could You teach Joseph not to argue with our teacher so he won't get in trouble?

"I want to live Your way because I know that's best. I think I'd like to be a doctor, but I know You have a plan for me and will help me make the right choices. Thank You for hearing and answering my prayers. Oh yeah, thanks for answering my prayer for Melissa. In Jesus' name, amen."

Encourage them to have new and relevant prayer requests in the different categories each night.

Faith Like George Mueller's

At the beginning of this section we mentioned the faith of George Mueller. In 1835, Europe had a multitude of orphans and not nearly enough orphanages to meet the need. Mueller believed that if a poor man of little means like himself could simply, by prayer and faith, obtain the means to establish and run an orphanage, it would strengthen the faith of the children of God.

Afterward he said about his motivation:

> I certainly did from my heart desire to be used by God to benefit the bodies of poor children, bereaved of both parents, and seek in other respects, with the help of God, to do them good for this life; I also particularly longed to be used by God in getting the dear orphans trained up in the fear of God; but still, the first and primary object of the work was (and still is) that God might be magnified by the fact that the orphans under my care are provided with all they need, only by prayer and faith, without anyone being asked by me or my fellow-laborers, whereby it may be seen that God is FAITHFUL STILL, and HEARS PRAYER STILL.[1]

George Mueller started with nothing but faith in God. He never asked anyone for a penny and refused to take a regular salary. In his lifetime he handled over eight million dollars, an enormous amount in the 1800s. Building from nothing, he soon ran five successful orphanages. By 1870, two thousand orphans were being cared for. George never incurred a single debt but daily relied on God to meet his needs and the needs of the orphanages.

Reading the carefully documented stories of God's miraculous and always timely provision, coming from people who had no idea of the current need, is faith inspiring. God never left them without. George didn't just trust God for money and the meeting of temporal needs. He prayed and trusted God for the right staff, the kids who came, and for the right running of the orphanages and the proper, natural, and spiritual education of the children. The quality of education was so high that George Mueller was accused of lifting the poor above their place in life and thereby taking laborers from the mines. Each orphan was trained in a trade or occupation and placed in a position upon leaving the orphanage. By 1880, besides the orphanages, George Mueller's organization was responsible for seventy-two day schools with seven thousand students in England, Italy, Spain, and South America. His organization would give away as many as one hundred thousand tracts and Bibles in a week. Through his visionary plans in England and other countries, tens of thousands of people became Christians.

Your children's prayers and a growing relationship with God can increase their faith and affect their world.

Yes, your children's prayers and a growing relationship with God can increase their faith and affect their world. George Mueller set out to show that God is living, that He answers prayer, and that He is faithful and can be trusted. His life and prayers demonstrated exactly that. The key for our children is that prayer be a foundation of their lives.

Abraham Lincoln used prayer as a last resort for most of his life. However, when he learned that prayer was to be his foundation and only trust, God used him and his prayers to help his country through one of its darkest hours. Likewise, George Washington Carver led a life of notable achievement because he knew from his youth that our relationship with God is central to who we are and how we are to live.

My prayer is that you will be George Mueller to your children, demonstrating and teaching them the purpose and possibilities of prayer. No matter where you or your children are today, I trust that, like Abraham Lincoln, God will move your family to a place where prayer is the foundation of your lives and your only trust. Finally, I pray that God will work with and in you and your children as you teach and as they learn so that your children, like George Washington Carver, will have a wonderful relationship with God and a life of notable achievement.

Questions

1. How is prayer like conversation? How is it different?

2. In your prayer life, do you tend to use written prayers or do you "freewheel" it on your own?

How about your children? What do they use?

3. What kinds of prayers could you incorporate into your and your children's prayer times to make them more well-rounded and effective?

_____

_____

4. In what situations might it be appropriate for you to use written prayers with your children?

_____

_____

_____

What situations are better suited to a "freewheel" approach?

_____

_____

_____

Prayer Checklist
- Talk to God every day, not just when you have a problem.
- Line up your prayers with who God is. (For example, don't ask God to be mean!)
- Pray for things the Bible says to pray for.
- Don't pray for what the Bible says not to pray for.
- Pray for God to do things according to His will, not yours. Trust Him, He knows a lot more than you do!
- How is your faith? If it's low, ask God to help you trust Him.
- Be thankful. God loves a thankful pray-er.
- Don't give up. Keep on praying no matter what. God is always working, even when you can't see it.

Don't Forget:
- Sin can come between you and God. When you pray, confess any sins you may have done (be specific) and ask forgiveness.
- Forgive people who have hurt you. Ask God to help you do this. He understands how much it hurts.

Ideas for Prayer

- Thank God for everything He has taught you about prayer from this book.
- Ask God to help you apply what you know in your own prayer life and in the lives of your children.
- Ask God to continually teach you and your children how to pray.

Prayer for Kids

Here is a sample prayer your children can use.

"Dear Father, thank You for teaching me how to pray. Thank You also for people who write down prayers that I can use. Help me to get better at prayer as I get older. In Jesus' name, amen."

---

1. George Mueller, *Answers to Prayer* (Chicago: Moody, n.d.), 10.

Welcome to the Family!

Heritage Builders™

Helping You Build a Family of Faith

We hope you've enjoyed this book. Heritage Builders was founded in 1995 by three fathers with a passion for the next generation. As a new ministry of Focus on the Family, Heritage Builders strives to equip, train, and motivate parents to become intentional about building a strong spiritual heritage.

It's quite a challenge for busy parents to find ways to build a spiritual foundation for their families—especially in a way they enjoy and understand. Through activities and participation, children can learn biblical truth in a way they can understand, enjoy—and *remember.*

Passing along a heritage of Christian faith to your family is a parent's highest calling. Heritage Builders' goal is to encourage and empower you in this great mission with practical resources and inspiring ideas that really work—and help your children develop a lasting love for God.

***

How to Reach Us

For more information, visit our Heritage Builders Web site! Log on to **www.heritagebuilders.com** to discover new resources, sample activities, and ideas to help you pass on a spiritual heritage. To request any of these resources, simply call Focus on the Family at 1-800-A-FAMILY (1-800-232-6459) or in Canada, call 1-800-661-9800. Or send your request to Focus on the Family, Colorado Springs, CO 80995. In Canada, write Focus on the Family, P.O. Box 9800, Stn. Terminal, Vancouver, B.C. V6B 4G3.

To learn more about Focus on the Family or to find out if there is an associate office in your country, please visit www.family.org

We'd love to hear from you!

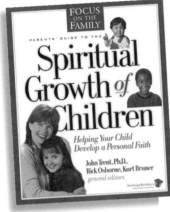

Parents' Guide to the Spiritual Growth of Children

Building a foundation of faith in your children can be easy–and fun!–with help from the *Parents' Guide to the Spiritual Growth of Children*. Through simple and practical advice, this comprehensive guide shows you how to build a spiritual training plan for your family and it explains what to teach your children at different ages.

My Time With God

Send your child on an amazing adventure— a self-guided tour through God's Word! *My Time With God* shows your 8- to 12-year-old how to get to know God regularly in exciting ways. Through 150 days' worth of fun facts and mind-boggling trivia, prayer starters, and interesting questions, your child will discover how awesome God really is!

The Singing Bible

Children ages 2 to 7 will love *The Singing Bible*, which sets the Bible to music with over 50 original, sing-along songs! *The Singing Bible* walks your child through the Old and New Testament Scripture. Introduce Adam and Eve in the Garden, the Ten Commandments, Jonah and the Whale, the Lord's Prayer, and many other biblical characters and facts in this four-cassette collection of songs that will have kids singing along! Memorable lyrics, tongue twisters, and an energetic narrator to guide them makes understanding the Bible an exciting journey.

Heritage Builders™

Helping You Build a Family of Faith

Bedtime Blessings

Strengthen the precious bond between you, your child, and God by making *Bedtime Blessings* a special part of your evenings together. From best-selling author John Trent, Ph.D., and Heritage Builders, this book is filled with stories, activities, and blessing prayers to help you practice the biblical model of "blessing." Designed for use with children ages 7 and under, *Bedtime Blessings* will help affirm the great love and value you and God have for your child, and will help each of your evenings together be filled with cherished moments in loving company.

Joy Ride!

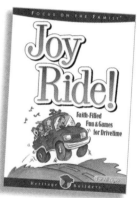

When you think of all the time kids spend in the car, it makes sense to use the time to teach lasting spiritual lessons along the way. *Joy Ride!* is a fun and challenging activity book that helps parents blend biblical principles into everyday life. Games, puzzles, Bible-quiz questions, and discussion starters give parents fun ways to get the whole family involved in talking and thinking about their faith. Make the most of your time together on the road with this fun, inspiring guide. Small enough to fit into a glove compartment, it's great for vacations *and* local trips!

An Introduction to Family Nights

Make devotions something your children will *never* forget when you involve them in "family nights"—an ideal way to bring fun and spiritual growth together on a weekly basis. *An Introduction to Family Nights* delivers 12 weeks' worth of tried-and-tested ideas, object lessons, and activities for helping kids learn how to tame the tongue, resist temptation, be obedient, and much more!

Heritage
Builders
Helping You Build a Family of Faith

Every family has a heritage—a spiritual, emotional, and social legacy passed from one generation to the next. There are four main areas we at Heritage Builders recommend parents consider as they plan to pass their faith to their children:

Family Fragrance

Every family's home has a fragrance. Heritage Builders encourages parents to create a home environment that fosters a sweet, Christ-centered AROMA of love through Affection, Respect, Order, Merriment, and Affirmation.

Family Traditions

Whether you pass down stories, beliefs, and/or customs, traditions can help you establish a special identity for your family. Heritage Builders encourages parents to set special "milestones" for their children to help guide them and move them through their spiritual development.

Family Compass

Parents have the unique task of setting standards for normal, healthy living through their attitudes, actions, and beliefs. Heritage Builders encourages parents to give their children the moral navigation tools they need to succeed on the roads of life.

Family Moments

Creating special, teachable moments with their children is one of a parent's most precious and sometimes, most difficult responsibilities. Heritage Builders encourages parents to capture little moments throughout the day to teach and impress values, beliefs, and biblical principles onto their children.

We look forward to standing alongside you as you seek to impart the Lord's care and wisdom onto the next generation—onto your children.

Heritage Builders™

Helping You Build a Family of Faith

L I G H T *wave*

building Christian faith in families

Lightwave Publishing is one of North America's leading developers of quality resources that encourage, assist, and equip parents to build Christian faith in their families. Their products help parents answer their children's questions about the Christian faith, teach them how to make church, Sunday school, and Bible reading more meaningful for their children, provide them with pointers on teaching their children to pray, and much, much more.

Lightwave, together with its various publishing and ministry partners, such as Focus on the Family, has been successfully producing innovative books, music, and games for the past 15 years. Some of their more recent products include the *Parents' Guide to the Spiritual Growth of Children, Mealtime Moments*, and *Joy Ride!*

Lightwave also has a fun kids' Web site and an Internet-based newsletter called *Tips and Tools for Spiritual Parenting*. For more information and a complete list of Lightwave products, please visit: **www.lightwavepublishing.com**

MOODY
The Name You Can Trust
A MINISTRY OF MOODY BIBLE INSTITUTE

Moody Press, a ministry of Moody Bible Institute, is designed for education, evangelization, and edification.

If we may assist you in knowing more about Christ and the Christian life, please write us without obligation:

Moody Press, c/o MLM Chicago, Illinois 60610.

Or visit us at Moody's Web site: **www.moodypress.org**